# SCREENWRITING and THE UNIFIED THEORY OF NARRATIVE

# SCREEN WRITING and THE UNIFIED THEORY OF NARRATIVE

PART I : THE UNIFIED NARRATIVE STRUCTURE

## MICHAEL WELLES SCHOCK

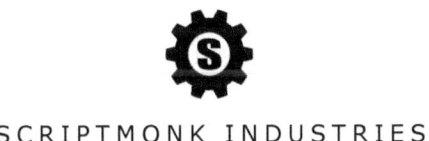

SCRIPTMONK INDUSTRIES

ISBN 978-0-9888487-3-3

First Edition

# CONTENTS

*In the land of the blind, the one-eyed man is king.*
*The two-eyed man is a pariah.*

# INTRODUCTION

Let me begin by stating that this is not a "How-to" book. It is not a production manual. It will not teach you how to start with a FADE IN and then construct a script page by page until it reaches the obligatory FADE OUT. Nor will it tell you how to write a "commercial screenplay" or a script guaranteed to sell (as if there was any way to predict such a thing). This is a book on theory.

What kind of theory? As far as screencraft is concerned, this book seeks the *theory of everything*. In its current state, the field of screencraft exists as a scattered collection of ideas and concepts, structures and models, odds and ends with no method to unite them into a single system of thought. In other words, screencraft is like a jigsaw puzzle with no guide as to how its pieces must fit together. While deconstructive analysis has broken down many narrative elements in detail, the power of cinematic storytelling is not found in its individual parts, but what happens when those parts are combined to create a singular story experience. No story succeeds by plot alone. Or by character. Or by theme or any other component. Storytelling is a cohesive experience where all elements come together as one. Screencraft cannot become a useful guide for the creation of new and original cinematic stories until it identifies the principles that act to unify the many narrative elements that until now have only been considered in separation. As such, this book aims to understand cinematic storytelling not in terms of its bits and pieces, but as a whole. It seeks the structure that unites all structures. A theory that will govern all theories. The method by which all other methods must abide. It provides a *unified* theory of narrative.

Needless to say, this is not a book for beginners. Though it strives to remain clear at all times, it assumes the reader already possesses a basic knowledge of screencraft. It also must be said that this book builds upon certain concepts introduced in my previous book *Screenwriting Down to the Atoms*. Whenever necessary, this text provides a brief overview of these concepts, but on the whole avoids overly-rehashing this material. For readers at the beginner or intermediate level, I suggest you first refer to my previous book or a similar text. (Alternatively, an abridged version of *Atoms* titled *Screenwriting Down to the Atoms: The Absolute Essentials* has been made available for free online.\* This four-chapter edition contains much of the requisite information. Please see the appendix on page 167 for more information.)

Given that a "theory of everything" (or as close as one can come to it at this current juncture) is a particularly lofty goal, some statements must be made on how this will be approached. Firstly, though this book focuses on theory, it is meant to provide *practical* theory. Quite often critical theory has no use outside of the debates of academia. In contrast, this book has been created as an active resource for cinematic storytellers. The concepts contained herein can and should be directly applied to one's own work. Though this book sometimes engages in the hypothetical and often jour- neys outside of the traditional boundaries of its subject matter, its primary goal is to help cinematic storytellers better understand their craft so they may produce better and more effective works of narrative.

Secondly, this book has no intention of inventing narrative formulas to be followed blindly. This book invents nothing. It only illuminates that which has developed naturally over the course of time in response to the valid physical factors of the cinematic medium, the psychological factors of the

---

\* For free or next-to-free. Some online retailers require a minimal service charge.

viewing audience, and the sociological factors that have shaped the cinematic story's manner and method of execution. No one invented these patterns or principles. They have not been artificially contrived and forced upon their medium. They are simply the natural result of a process of evolution and refinement that has occurred over the past century as the cinematic story has searched for its most effective shape, structure, and form.

Thirdly, in the pursuit of both truth and accuracy, the investigation and analysis contained in this book strives to abide as close as possible to academic methods of inquiry. For too long, writers on the subject have passed off opinion for fact, educated guesses for proven truth, ignored contrary evidence, and made universal declarations which do not have universal application. The investigation of screencraft will never be taken seriously until it adopts legitimate methods. This first means statements must be based upon sound logic and backed up by observable evidence. Furthermore, no concept should be taken for granted without thorough evaluation. Any evidence to the contrary must be investigated further. Exceptions should not be ignored as it is often the exceptions that reveal the truth. If logical reasons are found for the exception's deviation, then the proposition can be considered valid. If reasons for deviation cannot be found, the conclusion must be declared false or at best remain an incomplete hypothesis with clearly stated reservations.

With this in mind, it becomes important to consider which feature films this book uses as evidence to support its claims. It goes without saying that these films should be excellent examples of cinematic storytelling. However, the qualifications for "excellence" lack empirical standards. For the most effective substitute, I have selected films by the following criteria: First, the film must be popular. This means the film has been widely-seen and well-liked amongst a large enough portion of the population to achieve cultural status. Second, the film must have received positive critical recognition for its narrative qualities. While films that are popular are not always critically-approved, and those that are critically-approved are not always popular, this book finds the best of both categories by relying upon the percentage that meet both qualifications. Third, the film (with a few exceptions) must be at least ten years old. The ultimate test of quality is the ability to withstand the passage of time. Superior works of storytelling retain their recognition with passing years, while lesser works are forgotten. "Classic" films earn this status not simply because of their age, but because the strength of their storytelling allows them to remain relevant despite changes in audiences and social trends. One can see the effect of time upon even relatively-recent films. The *Dark Knight* and *Avatar* were the biggest box-office smashes of 2008 and 2009, respectively. Yet although *Avatar* outgrossed *The Dark Knight* at the box office, *The Dark Knight* has retained great popularity due to its superior storytelling while recognition for *Avatar* has faded quickly. With more time, *The Dark Knight* will likely achieve the status of a modern classic as *Avatar* recedes into distant memory.

Finally, a crucial disclaimer must be made. The concepts contained in this book were developed with an exclusive focus upon Hollywood and American Independent cinema. This was not done out of ethnocentrism or any belief that American cinema is superior to all others. Rather, this was done in recognition of the fact that stories exist as sociocultural artifacts that express the values and beliefs of the time and place from which they originate. Since values and beliefs differ from one culture to the next, so will the content and methods found in their storytelling. (This concept will be addressed in further detail in Part II of this book.) I was born in the United States and have lived my entire life within its borders. Therefore, I am best acquainted with American culture and its use of story. However, I will not be so arrogant to assume that I understand the people of any other nation well enough to apply my culturally-specific observations to the cinematic expressions of their countries as well. While many values and beliefs are shared across cultures, a comprehensive overview of global cinema lies outside the scope of this book as well as the experience of this author. At its furthest extent, my observations may also apply to the cinemas of other Anglicized English-speaking nations; such as Canada, Australia, New Zealand, and Great Britain; since these nations share cultural affinities due to their historical pasts and shared language. Yet even in these cases, strong reservations must be made. Though much expressed in this book may apply to all world cinema in general, I will leave it to more knowledgeable critics to investigate and adapt its methods to other national cinemas as best fit.

The art of storytelling has two primary functions. The first is to entertain an audience with a clear and dramatic narrative. The second and more significant function is to act as a carrier of sociocultural meaning. As such, this book has been presented in two sections. "Part I: The Unified Narrative Structure" presents the common method used by the feature-length film to combine its various narrative structures into a single and cohesive story experience. "Part II: Genre, Pattern, and the Concept of Total Meaning" explores the less readily-observable properties of the American feature film which, largely unbeknownst to the audience, provide the story with a greater sense of purpose and meaning.

Many of the following concepts are new to the field of screencraft. Some may run counter to the notions currently taught. However, it is only with an open mind and an intellectual enthusiasm that we may hopefully see through the clouds of confusion and find the most accurate and comprehensive understanding of our craft. With this, we will not only better understand our stories, but better understand ourselves; both as storytellers and collectively as a people.

# CHAPTER 1-1

# THE FAILURE OF SCREENCRAFT

In my experience, there are few ambitions filled with more confusion and frustration than that of the aspiring screenwriter. What begins as a dream to recreate the excitement found in the theater, or perhaps express oneself to the world in an equally powerful manner, soon runs into the realization that a great cinematic story requires far more than imagination. Just as a youngster who wishes to become an astronaut must learn this requires more than putting on a helmet and jettisoning into space; or one who dreams of being a rock star must find this requires more than the playing of an instrument; the aspiring screenwriter eventually discovers that successful cinematic stories require equal parts art and science. Cinematic storytelling is a complex and delicate thing. Due to numerous factors, it has more strictures and limitations imposed upon it than possibly any other form of expression. Composing a feature-length script that simply meets the requirements of its medium is a challenge. Creating one that also excites and entertains is an even greater one.

Most aspiring screenwriters respond to this challenge by seeking education. To meet the demand, an entire cottage industry of books, classes,

DVDs, and seminars has sprung up to serve this small but thriving market. Unfortunately, when aspirants attempt to apply this instruction to their own work, many end up more confused and frustrated than ever before. Because of this, some in the screenwriting community have developed the opinion that the men and women behind such materials (often referred to as "script gurus") are little more than snake oil salesmen. They promise to turn lead into gold, but cannot back up the claim. However, these negative opinions are largely unwarranted. The great majority of writer-analysts do their honest best to help young and developing writers. The problem simply arises from the fact that in its current state the field of screencraft is still *not yet ready* to do what it promises.

Though the modern study of cinematic storytelling has now existed for roughly forty years, the field is still stuck in its adolescence. Its theories remain incomplete and its methods immature. It has yet to reach a state where it understands the complexities of its own subject matter well enough to put this knowledge to direct use with consistent and reliable success. Due to this failure, the academic world has yet to fully recognize the study of the cinematic narrative as a serious field of inquiry. While the critical analysis of literature or theatrical drama have been long considered worthwhile endeavors, the storytelling found in movies is still treated as a silly or frivolous thing. This is unfortunate. As the now far-most dominant form of storytelling the world over, one which exerts a greater influence over a greater portion of the population than literature or theatre ever achieved at their heights, the stories found in cinema act as the most accurate expressions of the values, beliefs, concerns, and aspirations of our modern civilization. The cinematic story is indeed worthy of the same attention paid to literature or the theatre. Unfortunately, the road to legitimacy has been sidetracked by impatience and mismanaged priorities.

The history of screencraft presents a proverbial case of putting the cart before the horse. Any legitimate field of study has two general areas of emphasis: investigation and application. Investigation is deconstructive in nature. It breaks down complex, naturally-occurring systems of phenomena in order to extract the rules by which they function. Application is constructive in nature. It uses the discoveries of investigation to create something new and useful. Yet for application to achieve any real success, investigation must precede it by a wide margin. One cannot apply knowledge that one does not yet have. As an example, medicine in an applicative science. It aims to construct artificial treatments to ensure longer and healthier lives. However, without the investigative discoveries of biology and organic chemistry, medicine would have little to draw upon to achieve its intended purpose. Likewise, architecture is an applicative art. Yet architects would be unable to construct anything over a few meters tall if not for the investigative work of physics and mathematics that preceded it.

In the same way, the writing of a screenplay is a constructive endeavor. As an applicative art, competent screenwriting requires a certain bedrock of knowledge to first exist if it is to be undertaken with consistent and reliable success. Without sufficient knowledge, success can only come through trial and error, intuitive experience, or that rare and magical thing known as "raw talent."

In consideration of this, it can be rightly claimed that the writer-analysts of screencraft have jumped the gun. For the past forty years, the vast majority of materials on the subject have been in the form of "how-to" manuals. Do this, this, and this, they say and anyone can create a perfect screenplay. Unfortunately, these books do not come close to containing the quantity nor the quality of knowledge necessary to back up this claim. From the very start, writer-analysts have proceeded directly to application with only a meager amount of investigative knowledge to support it. Based on such weak foundations, all this instruction could provide was spotty evidence and premature conclusions, often held together by nothing more than rough theories or educated guesses. This explains much of the frustration developing screenwriters feel towards materials on the subject. They have been promised success, but have been given insufficient tools to attain it.

If the purpose of screencraft is to help young and developing writers create new and original cinematic stories through the application of practical knowledge, it cannot accomplish these aims until it completes its investigative role. So far, the investigation of screencraft has barely scratched the surface. Most of its teachings remain superficial in nature. The majority of screencraft's internal processes remain a mystery. Simply observing what lies on the surface is not enough. Nor is stopping with creative explanations which have the suggestion of truth but no factual basis. Like all other fields of inquiry, screencraft must look deep into the foundations of its subject matter and seek the answers to its most fundamental questions before it can hope to put its knowledge to any substantial use. Otherwise, the field remains inadequate and will continue to deserve its lack of recognition.

Some readers may feel uncomfortable with the idea of approaching cinematic storytelling in the same manner as a science. Many have been taught to believe art and science must be kept separate. However, storytelling is more than just an art. Though many people think of stories as little more than isolated acts of fantasy or entertainment, analysts of screencraft must recognize that the physical act of storytelling is part of a *naturally-occurring system of human phenomena* that has existed since the beginnings of mankind. Whenever and wherever human beings have congregated into groups of shared identity, storytelling has emerged. Every culture, modern or primitive, defines itself by a tradition of narrative. Human beings use story to make sense of their lives. This suggests that the telling and receiving of stories is natural and intuitive to our species, a universal impulse that most likely originates from basic psychological or sociological needs. This also suggests that storytelling must have a purpose. Human beings are fairly practical-minded creatures. We are planners and builders, a trait that has allowed our species to conquer the earth. Thus, it would be illogical to think that humanity would constantly create stories unless they served an important function. This means storytelling is not only a naturally-occurring phenomenon, but one that operates by principles orientated toward certain ends. Because of this, the process of storytelling can indeed be understood in the same manner as the investigative sciences. If we assume that stories emerge from the human mind in response to psychological or sociological needs, it can be claimed that storytelling is a systematic process motivated by comprehensible stimuli. If we make an effort to understand these stimuli and the processes by which narrative serves them, we can understand storytelling as well as we might any other naturally-occurring system of phenomena.

Yet still, many may resist this notion out of the belief that the act of storytelling contains certain ethereal qualities that can never be fully understood. We often hear of "the magic of storytelling" as if well-told stories have mystical properties originating from a supernatural source. However, a belief in magic has stood at the starting point of every legitimate area of human knowledge. From the rising of the sun to the birth of a child, humanity has originally assumed every naturally-occurring phenomenon to function by magic until investigative analysis uncovered the physical principles by which they actually operate. There is no such thing as magic. "Magic" is only a stand-in used for what we do not yet understand. As such, there is nothing truly magical about the process of storytelling. The effect may feel magical to the receiver, but the reason for this effect can be analyzed and understood. Through investigative analysis, storytelling can become demystified to a point where we not only understand this "magic," but can reproduce it on our own.

Unfortunately, little work has been done to unravel the mysteries of cinematic storytelling from the sociocultural perspective. The pioneers of this approach (such as structural anthropologist Claude Levi-Strauss and folklorist Joseph Campbell) focused their studies not on modern storytelling, but the myths and legends of pre-industrial societies. The founders of modern screencraft instead chose to follow a much different road,* one with both benefits and drawbacks that has led the field to the state it occupies today.

## THE CURRENT STATE OF SCREENCRAFT

Considering its forty years of existence, the modern study of cinematic storytelling has made relatively little progress. This sluggish development is largely due to its preferred method of analysis. Rather than investigate the

---

* With some exceptions; Christopher Vogler's loose adaptation of Campbell's theories being one example.

psychological or sociological properties of storytelling, the early writer-analysts chose to approach the subject through what is known as the Aristotelian method of inquiry. Named after the philosopher Aristotle, this method attempts to understand complex natural systems through categorization and organization. This is essentially a superficial approach based upon logic and observation. The first step is to group all perceivable elements of a system according to their observable similarities. Then, the method attempts to identify patterns and relationships between and among these groups through the search for invariants (qualities that remain constant from one instance to the next). If a pattern is found, the analyst can look closer at each element to identify its specific role or properties. When applied to screencraft, this approach relies mostly upon the comparison of existing films in a search for shared elements. If consistent similarities are found from one film to the next, the analyst proposes a narrative formula. (It is worth noting that Aristotle himself was the first to apply this method to the study of drama. His *Poetics*, written circa 335 BC is the first known work on dramatic theory.)

Taking inspiration from Aristotle, the early writer-analysts started with plot (the most visible element of dramatic storytelling) and identified a rough structural pattern repeated with relative consistency in films generally considered successful while missing from films considered failures.* Though still quite primitive, this rudimentary grasp of plot allowed writer-analysts to establish general principles of narrative structure. With this completed, writer-analysts felt comfortable moving on to the less tangible aspects of storytelling, such as character and theme. As more minds joined the hunt, the investigation of each element became more detailed and more sophisticated. After following this road for nearly four decades, deconstructive

---

\* It is worth noting that the study of screencraft began in earnest during the same period that saw the arrival of the first film school educated generation of filmmakers; a group that included Steven Spielberg, Martin Scorsese, George Lucas, and Francis Ford Coppola. Educated in both the traditional style of Classic Hollywood and the artistic experimentation of the New Wave period, this generation was set apart in that they did not seem to see themselves as engineers of spectacle or experimentive artists as had earlier generations, but instead embraced the role of master storytellers. With their emphasis on story, these filmmakers initiated the "blockbuster era" of Hollywood, creating films that received not only critical praise, but enormous commercial success. With this, Hollywood woke up to the importance of storytelling and its preeminent place in commercially successful film.

analysis has managed to disassemble the cinematic story as if it were a giant machine. Virtually every identifiable element has been broken down, scrutinized, debated, (all with varying degrees of insight or accuracy) and then assigned a specific role, property, or function.

Yet while the Aristotelian method proves quite adequate for analytic disassembly, it runs into major roadblocks if one attempts to use it for the creation of something new. The Aristotelian method is purely deconstructive. It was not designed for the constructive act of creation nor was this ever its intention. Its purpose is to analyze preexisting phenomena so one may formulate monotypical systems to predict natural occurrences in consistent ways. This first of all means it examines only end results, not the processes by which those results are created. It is investigative, not applicative. Secondly, it assumes that the phenomena encountered will always be the same and will always lead to the same results under the same circumstances. This makes it suitable for the study of the natural sciences, as the properties of natural phenomena never change. The process of artistic creation however could not have less in common with the consistent repetition found in nature. In fact, its intention is to invent something which has never existed before. Every cinematic story must contain new and unique content and therefore each must undergo a slightly different process in its telling. While the Aristotelian analysis of screencraft may have discovered general patterns within existing films which seem to generate consistent audience reactions, one cannot simply reverse this method and expect it to output original material equal in quality to the films analyzed. Aristotelian inquiry provides only a monotype. A monotype can only produce the same thing again and again without change or variation. Therefore, an Aristotelian system is quite possibly the worst tool one could use to create something new and unique. The two processes are completely unrelated and should have never been associated with one another.

Furthermore, young and developing screenwriters are often baffled upon encountering the results of Aristotelian deconstruction. Imagine if you will a giant machine which has been disassembled so that its hundreds of parts lay strewn across a factory floor. Now imagine if a novice machinist should enter the factory and be told he or she must put the machine back together again. The novice can only react with terror. He or she has NO CLUE how to do this. The novice barely knows how machines work, let alone how to make proper use of such a confusing array of parts. What is even worse, the novice is told he or she must not only assemble the machine, but a *new* machine that must perform tasks completely different than the original. This of course is all but impossible.

This is the current state of screencraft. We have learned a great deal by taking cinematic stories apart, but this has effectively left the field in shambles. Deconstruction may have satiated our intellectual curiosity, but it has yet to provide aspiring writers with what they need to create new and original work. Aspiring storytellers do not need to know how things are taken apart, but rather *how to put them together.*

This problem has been worsened by the fact that in the pursuit of analytic deconstruction the study of screencraft has become highly compartment-alized. For ease of study, the elements of plot, character, and theme have been analyzed in isolation. Open any book on the subject (my own previous book not withstanding) and you will surely find one section dedicated solely to plot, another solely to character, and yet another to theme (if the author has even bothered to discuss all three). While there are certainly good reasons to arrange material in such a way, this has given readers the inadvertent impression that dramatic elements exist independently from one another and operate in isolation. Compartmentalized analysis tends to promote the idea that plot, character, and theme are largely unrelated "lines" that may intersect or intertwine, but always remain separate and distinct. Yet all one must do is view a single well-made film to find this is patently untrue. Cinematic stories are not compartmentalized. Their content is holistic. Every element connects to everything else. A cinematic narrative contains a single line of action in which all dramatic elements meld together to form a seamless whole. When three streams join to create a single river, we do not see three separate currents, but one flowing entity. Likewise, a story should not be seen as a collection of parts. It is a process by which many elements combine to form a meaningful whole. If the investigation of screencraft intends to provide any real benefit to young and developing writers, it must shift its focus away from how individual elements work to how they work together.

As such, screencraft now stands at a crucial turning point in its development. We have taken the cinematic story apart and have learned a great deal in the process. But now comes the time to put Humpty-Dumpty back together again. To turn our deconstructive knowledge into anything of practical use, we must now identify what principles unify the craft's many concepts into a single functional system. Thus, the study of screencraft must transition into its second phase of analysis: *re*-construction. It is no longer a question of how dramatic elements work, but how they work *together*. To find our answers, we must reevaluate our previous discoveries from a macroscopic level. We must look not only at the concepts themselves, but the greater psychological and sociological factors that explain why these concepts are necessary and why they are effective as opposed to other possible means. Storytelling has a purpose. The components of narrative serve this purpose, not individually, but in combination. A dissected animal is a dead animal. So is a dissected film. Yet when a cinematic story's many elements are combined with the correct balance and order, the story finds not only its cohesion, but its life, its vibrancy, and its powerful effect upon the viewer.

The remainder of this book (both Parts I & II) seeks the principles that will unify screencraft once more. With this knowledge, we may come as close as possible to the sorcerer's stone writer-analysts have sought for decades: a comprehensive and potentially universal model which will explain the external and internal workings of the cinematic story in their entirety. Once attained, screencraft can finally come full circle and accomplish its originally-stated goal. Deconstructive investigation can finally lead to constructive application. Analysis can finally become a guide for creation.

# CHAPTER 1-2
## FROM STORY TO STRUCTURE:
# THE ORIGINATING PRINCIPLES

Let us begin by establishing that, on its most basic level, the cinematic film exists as a complex act of communication. All forms of storytelling communicate. This is their primary purpose. The same can be said for every art. Art is expressive in nature. It exists to communicate thoughts, ideas, and emotions to the world. This defining factor separates works of art from all other man-made objects. This communication does not occur directly however, but through a creative medium. An art may use words, sounds, or images to communicate. It may be composed of shapes, movements, colors, or any combination of elements. Whatever the case, the "medium" occupies the middle ground between artist and audience. It provides the substance through which communication travels. While many of the arts also entertain or provide aesthetic beauty, these goals are secondary in nature. The art merely uses such means to engage an audience's attentions so communication may occur.

Whether it be a high-minded museum piece or the purest of pop culture drivel, every work of creation communicates something. Even when an artist has no intention to communicate, expression will still occur. Every creative decision will be intuitively shaped by the artist's personal values, tastes, opinions, and beliefs. These decisions will in turn express something about the way the artist sees the world. Likewise, the audience often receives this communication without its explicit knowledge. While experiencing the work, usually as entertainment or an appreciation of beauty, the audience inevitably undergoes a process of thought and emotion that (consciously or not) leads it to certain conclusions. The message encountered may be extremely simple or very complex. It may express an entire ideology or a single emotion. Its meaning may be overt or hidden deep in subtext. Nevertheless, some form of meaning is transmitted from artist to audience, fulfilling the work's primary function.

Methods of communication vary greatly by medium. A traditional feature-length film communicates primarily through narrative. Like literature or theatrical drama, cinematic communication establishes a fictionalized situation in which characters encounter a problem. Meaning is ultimately expressed by how or if this problem is resolved. However, due to differences in their form and presentation, the cinema, literature, and theatre communicate their stories in very different ways. The novel can only communicate through written words. The stage play is limited to live dramatic reenactment. In comparison, the feature film's method of delivery is far more complex. The cinematic medium tells stories through the pre-recordal of dramatic reenactment, which is then manipulated through editing and presented to its audience at a far later time. This process is unique to the cinema, and therefore gives cinema special physical properties found in no other medium. Some of these properties work to cinema's advantage, allowing it to communicate in ways literature and theatre cannot. Others work to cinema's disadvantage, creating limitations not found in its contemporaries. In short, cinematic communication is governed by the physical factors of its medium. Its ideal method of storytelling is determined by what its medium can and cannot do.

It took filmmakers many years to figure out how to put cinema's unique qualities to their best use. Films from the earliest of decades seem strange or childish by today's standards as filmmakers had yet to discover the proper aesthetic language necessary to communicate successfully through image, montage, and (much later) sound. Some of these early films tried to copy the theatre. Others tried to imitate literature. But neither of these older methods were a proper fit. Eventually, through trial and error, innovation and experimentation, the cinema "found itself." It developed into its own form of artistic communication, one with a unique style that took full advantage of the medium's strengths and avoided its limitations.

To truly understand modern screencraft, one must first understand these strengths and limitations. The foundations of cinematic storytelling have been built upon the unavoidable consequences of its medium's physical properties. While some resist or criticize the study of screencraft because they consider its rules too rigid, it must be conceded that this rigidity is in fact an absolute necessity. The rules of screencraft exist in direct relation to the strengths and limitations of the cinematic form. What can or cannot be done in a feature length film has not been decided by analysts or critics, but by the properties of the medium itself.

## THE BOUNDARIES OF CINEMATIC STORYTELLING

Of the many physical limitations imposed upon the feature film, three are most relevant to screencraft: the feature film's prescribed length, the concept of verisimilitude, and the distance between story and audience.

When an author has a story to tell, he or she has the freedom to decide whether it is best told in a single paragraph or a thousand-page novel. A composer can express him or herself with anything from a ten-second melody to a three-hour symphony. In the same way, a painter may choose a canvas as large as a building or as small as a postage stamp. The feature-length cinematic storyteller has far less freedom. By industry standards, a feature film must run between 81-129 minutes.* This length is actually somewhat arbitrary. In cinema's formative years, filmmakers experimented

---

* Traditionally, that is. Films may run much longer, but these are usually considered special cases.

with all manner of lengths until it was concluded that audiences found this span of time most satisfactory – long enough to be worth the price of a ticket, yet not so long that the film became tiresome. With this, the feature film lost the structural freedom possessed by the novel. A preset length meant the cinematic narrative must follow structures optimized for this length. It also required that writers create stories with just the right amount of content to fill this window of time. Put too much content into the narrative and the story will be dense, rushed, or confused. Put in too little and the film will be dull or slow-moving. What dramatists now regard as cinematic story structure originally evolved out of the need to keep the story moving at a proper pace, one the audience could follow without becoming bored or confused.

Ironically, cinematic storytelling's second limitation is also its greatest strength: Verisimilitude. Verisimilitude is defined as the appearance of being true or real. When applied to art, this term refers to how closely the work imitates reality as we see, hear, or feel it. A painting done in a style realistic enough to be mistaken for a photograph has a high level of verisimilitude, while one in a formalist style has a verisimilitude which is very low. The storytelling arts vary in their capability to reproduce reality. Most require some use of imagination on the part of the audience to complete the illusion. Novels ask readers to visualize the characters, settings, and actions described. The viewers of a stage play must forget they are gazing at a cardboard backdrop on a raised platform and pretend the setting is real. Cinema on the other hand is unique among the arts in its ability to reproduce something that both looks and sounds as close to reality as an artificial creation can get. The motion picture camera is able to record anything a real eye might see and the microphone anything a real ear might hear. Through these tools, the cinema does not so much seem to imitate reality, but present something which appears real in itself.

Since the cinema presents something nearly indistinguishable from that which is real, its stories, though artificial, possess the *illusion* of physical actuality. This is what gives cinema its immersive, almost hypnotic quality. The illusion of actuality provokes the audience to "suspend its disbelief" so it may momentarily accept what it sees and hears as reality itself. Even when films depict a fantasy world or one containing highly unreal events, camera and sound still provide a tangible substance that the audience accepts as real despite the obvious fictionality of its content. Hence cinema's ability to make us believe anything. No matter how fantastic the story's events, film's verisimilitude allows us to accept them as readily as anything around us.

Yet while verisimilitude is the cinema's most powerful attribute, it is also its greatest handicap. Due to its reliance on sight and sound, the cinema can only communicate through what can be presented visually on screen or recorded onto the soundtrack. Any information that cannot be presented through these methods will never reach the audience. In comparison, literature has no such limitations. Literature can communicate anything at any time. It can provide information with the simple addition of a sentence. It can communicate the unseen thoughts and feelings of characters without the need for physical evidence. While literature cannot imitate reality in the same way as cinema, it is allowed a nearly unlimited ability to communicate, whereas the cinema is tightly restricted in this area.

Secondly, by imitating reality, cinematic stories are bound to the physical rules of reality. The content of the cinematic story must abide by the rules of space, time, and logic. Should any material run counter to reality as we know it, the illusion of actuality will be lost. Even when fantasy or science fiction films present worlds different than our own, the story world's deviations from reality must be clearly established up front and strictly adhered to throughout in order to maintain the audience's suspension of disbelief. Yet even in these cases, the deviations are few. The remainder of reality's rules remain constant in order to anchor the story in the realm of plausible actuality.

It is in this aspect that literature and the theatre have many advantages over cinema. With their lower degrees of verisimilitude, their stories may exist in worlds that are vague or abstract, or occupy realms where time, space, and logic have no meaning. A novel or short story may not exist in reality at all, but rather a psychological or emotional space where anything is possible. In similar fashion, the theater can turn its artificiality to its advantage through the use of formalist sets and costumes, unrealistic performances, or absurd premises which may enhance its capacity for expression in ways that would never be passable in the hard reality of the cinema.

These mismatches in verisimilitude are the reasons why so many of our greatest novels and plays can never be adapted into films with equal success. The works of Shakespeare always fall flat when turned into motion pictures, as the Bard's manner of discourse seems unnatural when matched with the realism of the cinema. Many masterpieces of literature will never find adequate cinematic counterparts, as their greatness is often based in literary qualities which cannot be reproduced through the limits of sight and sound. As this suggests, cinema's inescapable verisimilitude, while a golden boon for its aesthetic potential, acts as a prison for its narrative possibilities by placing hard rules upon what its stories can and cannot do.

Yet while a film has the appearance of reality, it is not a reality the audience can experience directly. The cinematic audience is distanced from the story in ways more profound than that found in literature or the theatre. In literature, the narrator speaks directly to the reader. It communicates by way of a one-way dialogue, often enhanced by the use of the first-person "I" voice, an effect nearly impossible to imitate in film. In theatre, the action takes place in the physical space directly in front of the viewer. The characters exist in their midst, almost close enough to touch. Plays often take their physical presence even further with dramatic devices intended to directly involve the audience in the story's discourse. The cinematic audience, on the other hand, can only experience the story as third-person voyeurs. This is the cinematic narrative's third limitation. It is as if the four sides of the screen were a window through which the audience must peer like peeping toms in order to view a distinctly-separate world on the other side. The audience cannot directly participate in the story's action. They can only observe it from afar.

Furthermore, though cinematic stories unfold in the present tense, the audience is left with the awareness that they are viewing something "old." The film's events have already been acted out to their completion and then "canned" onto celluloid or video for the audience to view at a later time. This is not the case in the live action of the theatre, nor is this sensation present in the voice of the narrator in literature. Therefore, the cinema also lacks immediacy. The cinematic audience is removed from the story not only by space, but also by time.

This distance between story and audience creates problems in the cinema. Primarily, to maintain its illusion of reality, the cinematic story must act as if its audience does not exist. It cannot acknowledge its audience, as this would disrupt verisimilitude.* Characters and events must seem to exist for their own sake, living in their own self-contained worlds separate from that of the viewer. As such, the story should hold the illusion of a documentary artifact. The rise and fall of events must appear to occur on its own accord to suit its own purposes, and would have done so even if a camera was not present to record it.

This creates a paradox in cinema's narrative discourse. As an art, cinema exists to communicate meaning. But how can a film open a dialogue with its audience when the story must act as if the audience does not exist? Furthermore, how can story events directly engage the thoughts and emotions of the audience if the audience must be relegated to the position of third-person voyeurs?

## THE PROCESS OF NARRATIVE COMMUNICATION

Since the cinematic story cannot speak directly to its audience, communication must occur through indirect means. This process contains a certain degree of abstraction, so the best way to understand it is to start with simplified examples. In this case, we will begin with one of the simplest forms of storytelling: the fable.

---

* Some films will occasionally use postmodern devices to "break the fourth wall" in order to speak directly to the audience. However, this does not provide direct communication, only the false illusion of it. Ironically, these devices are not meant to heighten the audience's connection with the story but to intentionally forefront the artificiality of the narrative.

Fables are contrived to communicate basic moral lessons. These tales use simplified characters (usually animals or one-dimensional human caricatures) to symbolize specific aspects of human behavior. The story then places these characters into scenarios where these behaviors lead to positive or negative outcomes. These outcomes provide the story's message. Take for example Aesop's "The Grasshopper and the Ant": The Ant spends the summertime hard at work, gathering and storing food. Meanwhile, the Grasshopper fritters time away having fun. The Grasshopper mocks the Ant for working so hard at a time when food is plentiful. Yet when winter comes, the Grasshopper is proved a fool. With no food to be found, the Grasshopper pays the price for its indolence while the Ant is rewarded for its industry. This story tells us that discipline is a virtue. If we work hard now, we will be ready when challenges come in the future. This message is not stated directly. The fable *translates* the elements of this message into representational forms. The Ant represents discipline. The Grasshopper represents frivolity. The coming of winter represents the inevitable challenges that will arrive with the passage of time. While on its surface this fable seems to be little more than an amusing tale of two insects, the story holds a deeper and more significant purpose. Every element has been specifically chosen to communicate a lesson by indirect means.

The cinematic story must operate in the same manner. It communicates by first translating each aspect of its meaning into representative characters and events. The physical elements of a story act as manifestations of meaning through which abstract ideas find tangible form and substance. Since these elements are solid and real, they can be observed and understood by the audience. While the audience absorbs the action on the story's surface, they unknowingly receive the story's ideological communication through it. Like in the fable, the audience observes how certain character behaviors lead to positive or negative outcomes. Using simple cause and effect logic, the audience is led to rational conclusions regarding the abstract concepts those behaviors are meant to represent.

As we can see, a story's characters and events act as symbolic stand-ins (or as a code, if you will) for the indirect expression of meaning. While the audience may believe it is simply watching a piece of entertainment, behind each character, action, or event lies a shadow of meaning. These many separate physical elements combine and interact to communicate the story's underlying message. Therefore, communication and entertainment are not exclusive from one another. They work together. A good cinematic story entertains through what it uses to communicate and communicates through what it uses to entertain, creating a double-articulation of meaning; one on the surface, one hidden in subtext. Through such double-articulation, *Back to the Future* is not only a tale of a young man trapped in the past, but also a lesson on how individuals must take responsibility for their own futures. *The Godfather* is not just a story on life in a mafia family, but also a parable on where to draw the line between ethics and survival. *Rocky* presents not only a story of a boxer, but an illustration on how one may gain a proper sense of self-worth.* With this approach, these stories fulfill their artistic function of ideological communication without violating the story's illusion of reality. Characters and events exist separately from the audience on one level, yet speak directly to them on another.

Oddly enough, this process of communication is not always conscious on the part of the storyteller. Often, the storyteller is merely trying to entertain. Yet as stated earlier, every story communicates something whether the storyteller is aware of it or not. This is because the process of storytelling operates by many of the same principles as a dream. When a dreamer sleeps, the subconscious mind takes the wants, needs, fears, and anxieties of waking life and translates them into physically-observable actions and images. Abstract thoughts and emotions are given shape and form through symbolic stand-ins. A fear becomes a monster. A worry becomes a pool of quicksand. The feelings, desires, and preoccupations which the waking mind cannot find means to express are easily transformed into visual representations by the subconscious. A similar process occurs in the formation of stories. The storyteller's underlying values, beliefs, fears, and aspirations prompt him or her to select story content that acts to represent these psychological preoccupations in tangible form. Often the storyteller is not aware of why

* See Chapter 1-6 for more on these films and the messages conveyed.

he or she chose a particular subject matter. The storyteller simply feels "drawn to it." Nevertheless, the storyteller expresses his or her values, ideas, and beliefs by encoding them into representational forms.

While dreams express the underlying anxieties and preoccupations of an individual dreamer, a culture's most popular stories collectively express the underlying wants, needs, fears, and aspirations of a population as a whole. As members of their culture or society, storytellers naturally share many of the same values and beliefs of those around them. When storytellers express themselves through narrative, the audience recognizes many of their own values, beliefs, fears, and aspirations therein. When we say an audience "identifies" with a film, this means viewers recognize a part of themselves within it. These stories become popular because their codes adequately address some aspect of the population's broad psychological needs, whether this is realized or not. Therefore, popular stories can be thought of as the collective dreams of a society at large. Great storytellers simply do through effort what the dreamer's mind does automatically.

However, dreams provide a chaotic and confusing experience. Rarely does one wake from a dream with any sense of what it might mean. In both story and in dreams, the receiver can only grasp some sense of meaning if the content is delivered with a clear order and coherent logic. Furthermore, proper narrative communication requires a great deal of skill. Meaning must be there, but not overtly. It must be present at all times, yet stay hidden behind the very devices used to communicate it. A good story must perform a balancing act between entertainment and communication so that the message does not distract from the entertainment nor the entertainment from the message. If communication is to occur in a manner that is clear and effective yet not overt, the narrative must develop according to some form of *structure*.

Generally speaking, a "structure" is a system of order found within the elements of a narrative. Key elements are established at the outset. These elements interact, creating a series of outcomes based upon the logic of cause and effect. This action eventually leads to a conclusion that provides the receiver with a sense of cognitive closure by resolving all narrative issues in a satisfactory manner. Structure makes a story clear and easy to understand. An audience grasps a story's meaning only when it can comprehend the logic connecting its events. Without structure, a story provides nothing but the unorganized confusion of a dream, rendering it unable to communicate any coherent meaning.

Very short forms of narrative can get by with a minimal amount of structure. The longer and more complicated the narrative, the greater the structural need. This is for two reasons. Firstly, the story contains more information and thus requires more organization. Secondly, a longer story must contend with the limits of the human attention span. Human attentions are surprisingly short. The longest forms of narrative such as novels, multi-act stage plays, and feature-length films must reinvigorate audience interest at regular intervals or else the story will quickly reach a point where the audience is no longer receptive. Narrative structures organize story content into a form that acts to continually reengage audience interest before it has a chance to wane. This way, the receiver remains attentive and open to further communication. (Details on this structural organization can be found in the next chapter.)

Long-form narratives must also deal with an additional structural problem. The further a story expands in length, the more it must also expand in *breadth*. Stories are like rivers. The longer the river, the broader its banks. Weak screenplays or manuscripts are often criticized for being "too thin." They meet the proper requirements for length, but do not seem to have enough meat on their bones to provide a full and satisfying experience. A "thin" story is one with a focus too narrow or content too one-dimensional to hold the audience's attention for an extended length of time. While its content may be sufficient for a shorter story, the material grows weak or tedious when stretched out for too long. But what is narrative breadth and where does it come from? Contrary to what many amateurs assume, narrative breadth is not achieved by adding more content to the plot. This makes the story denser, not broader. Breadth can only be achieved by expanding the exploration of story content into *multiple narrative dimensions*.

# THE DIMENSIONS OF NARRATIVE

The cinematic story is primarily composed of three narrative dimensions: plot, character, and theme. Not coincidentally, these dimensions correspond with the audience's three sets of psychological needs: the intellectual, the emotional, and the ideological. To satisfy an audience, a story must first fulfill intellectual needs: Is the story interesting? Does it make sense? Does it make viewers want to know how events will be resolved, and then answer their questions in a satisfactory manner? Secondly, a story should fulfill emotional needs: Does the story make the audience feel anything? Do they care about the characters' plight? Do events trigger a physiological response? Finally, a story should serve ideological needs: Does the story have a point? Does it mean anything? Does it seem to have a worth or value that extends beyond the events of the narrative itself? While a story can achieve a certain limited satisfaction by appealing to only one of these needs, an ideal story will meet the requirements of all three. This is largely accomplished by developing story content along all three narrative dimensions in equal measure. Generally speaking, the dimension of plot fulfills the audience's intellectual needs, the dimension of character the emotional needs, and the dimension of theme the ideological. When combined, the story becomes "three-dimensional." Viewing the film becomes a far more substantial experience as it fulfills not just one, but all three psychological appetites.

The relationship between plot, character, and theme is best explained by an analogy. Consider the concept of the human self. What makes up a human being? This is a fairly complicated question, as a conclusive answer must explain not only what we are, but how we think, how we act, and why we behave in this way. The human self is a complex thing. This originates from the fact that like a story, it is also composed of three interrelated dimensions: that of the body, the mind, and the "soul."

Our first dimension of self is that of our physical body; our mass, our weight, our visible appearance, the material space we occupy within our environment. The body is solid, real, and observable. It DOES things in a materially substantial way. It can move about and influence the world around it. Our bodies root us to a specific place and time and give us a vehicle to achieve our needs. Yet a body alone does not make a human being. The body is only a shell. A corpse has a body, but with nothing left to cause it to think and feel, it can no longer be called a human being, only the remains of one.

For a body to function, it requires the second dimension of self: the mind. Without the mind, the actions of the body have no source or meaning. Intangible yet undeniably real, the mind supplies the thoughts, desires, and emotions which motivate the body to act. No action is committed for its own sake. Physical actions are simply the tools used by the mind to accomplish its greater wants and needs. But the mind is more than the operating system of the body. It is also the seat of personal identity. It determines how we see ourselves, how we see others, and how we see our place in the world. It gives us a personality. It decides who we are, how we act, and what we would like to be.

Still, a body plus a mind does not equal a human being. This simply describes an animal. Animals think and act, but this is the limits of their existence. Animals do not care about, or even seem to comprehend, anything beyond their immediate wants or needs. Humans stand apart from the animals by their ability to see the world in terms beyond face value. Our advanced brains allow us to assign *meaning*. We do not merely think in terms of what is or what is not, but also what is "good" or what is "bad," what is "right" or what is "wrong," what has value or what does not. Simply put, human beings are able to *believe in things*. This adds moral and ethical dimensions to human nature. Animals do not judge their behavior. A tiger does not feel guilty for killing a deer. Nor does a rabbit feel shame for its cowardice. Humans, on the other hand, believe that behaviors should be governed by higher concepts external to themselves. For the lack of a better term, we will call this part of the human self the soul.

Spiritual implications aside, a soul can be thought of as the collection of values, beliefs, attitudes, and ideas one has internalized as a guide for behavior. One might call this a conscience, but the contents of the soul extend far beyond a conception of good and evil or right and wrong. The soul includes every concept relevant to the personal assignment of value or meaning. It decides how we interpret the world and the importance we attach to people, objects, and events. When the soul is added to the mind and body, we find that human behavior operates by a linear structure. The soul counsels the decisions of the mind; the mind then commands the actions of the body. Physical actions may be the expressions of the mind, but they originate from the values and ethics held within the individual's soul.

In conclusion, the human self exists as a trinity. Three separate dimensions (one physical, one present yet intangible, and one completely abstract) operate in harmony to form a single living, thinking, feeling human being. The self is three separate parts unified in a single entity.

Story, with its three dimensions of plot, character, and theme, operates in the same way. The plot provides the story with a "body." Like the human body, the plot has a physically-observable presence. Plot events DO things in a materially substantial way. Plot acts and moves. It creates moments of change that influence the world around it. Its action and conflict give the story the appearance of a living, breathing thing. Yet plot alone does not create a story. A story that is just plot is a hollow shell. Events may occur, but without something behind those events to give them purpose or meaning, the plot will make little sense and give the audience no reason to care. To give purpose to the body, a story must have a mind.

A story's "mind" is found in the dimension of character. No plot action occurs for its own sake. Behind every action are the personal wants and needs of individual characters. Characters give actions meaning. If the audience can understand the thoughts and emotions of characters, they will understand why actions are committed and what they are meant to achieve. But just as the human mind is more than the operating system of the body, characters are far more than the operators of plot. Characters give a story a sense of identity. Most stories revolve around a single character with a unique personality. By focusing on this character and his or her wants, needs, fears, and limitations, the story turns the cold and purely functional mechanizations of plot into something intimate and personal. The story is no longer about the events, but how those events affect this individual human being. This adds an emotional element to the story experience, fulfilling the audience's second set of psychological needs.

Yet plot and character do not complete a story. A story that is just plot and character lives the limited existence of an animal. It is born and then it dies, with nothing significant accomplished in between. Such a story lacks a reason to exist and does little more than take up the audience's time. To provide any real purpose or meaning, a story must have a "soul." This soul is found in the story's thematic dimension. Like the human soul, the theme is composed of the values, beliefs, attitudes, and ideas that govern how the story sees the world. It is what the story "believes in" and makes an effort to express through its narrative. Just as the human soul allows us to see the world in terms beyond face value, the theme provides a meaning and significance that extends beyond the physical content of the plot. Thus, the thematic dimension fulfills the audience's ideological needs. The story is not solely about what is or what is not, but something of greater value or meaning.

As we can see, the cinematic story also operates as a trinity. Three narrative dimensions (one physical, one present but with intangible qualities, and one abstract) work in harmony to create a single unified story. Just as the body, mind, and soul depend on one another to function; plot, character, and theme cannot create a story on their own. Theme by itself is nothing more than a philosophical argument; ideas without substance. Character on its own provides only a psychological profile; thoughts and emotions without actions to fulfill them. Plot by itself is nothing but a record of chronological events; actions without meaning. The cinematic story works only when its three dimensions interact to form a single package. It is through this multidimensional interaction that the audience not only comprehends the story, but grasps its greater meaning. Just as one can discover the contents of an individual's soul by first observing the actions of the body and through them ascertain the thoughts and emotions of the person's mind, an audience can observe the actions of a story's plot, understand them through character, and from this discover the theme.

Yet, as already stated, the only way for an audience to make sense of these dimensions is if their content is delivered with some sort of structure. Meaning can only be grasped if accompanied by coherency and order. Cinematic storytelling has developed specialized structures of plot, character, and theme that act to fulfill each dimension's essential functions while meeting the unique requirements of the feature-length cinematic form. These structures will be explained in the following chapter. Once established, later chapters will explore the means by which these structures interact to form a cohesively unified cinematic narrative.

# CHAPTER 1-3
# THE COMPONENTS

Narrative structures are organized processes of CHANGE. In the cinematic narrative, change is the only constant. Events continually move forward. Action always progresses. This is a property of the medium itself. Time constantly advances when viewing a film, both on screen and in the experience of the viewer. Even when characters stand still, the narrative continues to progress. Nothing that constantly moves forward can ever stay the same. Movement means change. Likewise, all content within a cinematic narrative exists in a never-ending state of transition. This is the case for all three dimensions of storytelling: plot, character, and theme.

Because of their constant forward movement, narrative structures are commonly visualized as journeys with beginnings and ends. As such, the cinematic story is composed of three simultaneous journeys; a physical journey composed of plot events, a psychological journey taking place within the story's main character, and an ideological journey through which the story explores its theme. Formally, these structures are known as the STORY SPINE, the CHARACTER ARC, and the THEMATIC ARGUMENT.

(Note: Some of what follows might be considered basic review. Though the reader may already possess this knowledge, it is important to reestablish these fundamental principles before moving on. To avoid repetition, I will provide only an overview of the Story Spine and Character Arc, as these concepts have already been discussed in detail in my previous book. If you require more information, it can be found in the free abridged version, *Screenwriting Down to the Atoms: The Absolute Essentials.*\*)

## THE STORY SPINE

Though I often use the two terms interchangeably, there is a profound difference between a *story* and that which can only be considered a *narrative*. "Narrative" is a far broader term. At its simplest, a narrative need be nothing more than a series of events related in linear order. "I took off my shoes; I changed my socks; I put my shoes back on" is a narrative. So is "Abraham begot Isaac, who then begot Jacob." But neither of these constitutes a story. A "story" possesses specific qualities to distinguish it from a simple string of events. My previous book defines a story as such: a story is a series of events, a) about *characters* b) dealing with a *problem,* c) unified by a *premise,* and d) told in a *structured order.* Any narrative that does not meet these four basic requirements is not a story and will lack the ability to hold audience interest for an extended length of time.

The Story Spine is the structure that turns a narrative *into* a story. It organizes narrative content to meet story's four basic requirements while giving that content a clear focus and direction. The Story Spine does this by establishing the five basic components of plot:

a. The Story Problem
b. The Story Goal
c. The Path of Action
d. The Source of Main Conflict
e. The Stakes

These components can be visualized by the following diagram:

---

\* Please refer to page 167 for a partial list of online distributors.

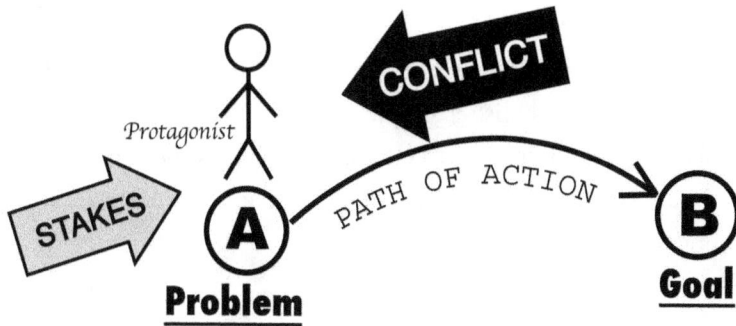

The Story Spine is not unique to cinema. Nor is it anything new. The Story Spine is as old as storytelling itself. For centuries on end, all well-told stories, from epic novels to tales told at the campfire, have provided their audiences with clear and compelling experiences by adhering to this structure's basic form. This is chiefly because a worthwhile story must abide by certain fundamentals of plot if it hopes to engage and then maintain audience attention. Along with fulfilling the four qualifications of story, the components of the Story Spine also establish a structure that meets these fundamental needs. First of all, a story must be about the pursuit of an objective. This pursuit gives a story movement, clarity, and purpose by concentrating all narrative content upon what characters want to achieve and the actions they take to do so. Without an objective, the best a story can provide is a wandering chain of pointless events lacking any unifying purpose or goal. However, there must be a legitimate reason for this pursuit. The audience must understand why characters take action and what meaningful result this pursuit hopes to achieve. In other words, the story must not only be going somewhere, but for a darn good reason. Without such logic to back up the story's action, narrative events will make little sense and hold no actual meaning. Furthermore, there must be some question regarding whether or not the characters will succeed. The concept of doubt is essential to an engaging story. Audiences remain attentive out of a desire to know how events will be resolved. If they can predict results ahead of time, there will be no incentive for continued interest. Therefore, a story must keep its outcome uncertain by including elements that may prevent the objective from being reached.

Together, the Story Problem, Story Goal, Path of Action, Source of Main Conflict, and Stakes establish a simple structure that meets these fundamental narrative requirements in a clear and logical manner, creating a plot with focus, movement, and meaning; one that is not only entertaining, but easy to understand.

## The Story Problem

At their heart, all stories are about problems and the search for a solution. This is for reasons both functional and sociological in nature. On a functional level, dramatic action cannot occur until characters are motivated to act. Objectives are not pursued unless there is a reason. By inserting a major problem into characters' lives, the story gives the characters a legitimate cause to take action. Whether the Story Problem be something small and personal or large and life-threatening, its arrival acts to light a fire under the protagonist,* forcing him or her to do what is necessary to resolve the situation.

On a sociological level, stories use a dramatic process of problem-solving as a way to express meaning. Stories suggest the "right" way for individuals to behave by demonstrating how proper actions and behaviors can fix something which has gone "wrong." Conversely, a story can also warn viewers away from improper behaviors by showing how those behaviors fail to solve problems, create new problems, or make problems worse.

For these reasons, a story does not officially begin until a) the protagonist encounters the Story Problem, and then b) decides to do something about it. In screencraft, this moment is known as the Inciting Incident ("incite" meaning to rouse to action). This Story Problem must be significant enough to disrupt the protagonist's life and prevent him or her from pursuing any unrelated objectives until a solution is found. The problem *must* be taken care of, right *now*. Due to this urgency, the Story Problem becomes the

---

* The term "protagonist" refers to the story's central character. The name is derived from Greek, meaning "first actor."

central focus of the story's forthcoming actions. All narrative events will revolve around the consequences of the Story Problem and the protagonist's quest for a resolution.

## The Story Goal

No problem can be solved without a plan. To make any headway, the protagonist must aim for a clear and definite resolution. The Story Goal is a specific objective that the protagonist believes, if accomplished, will resolve the Story Problem and return life to what he or she wishes it to be. Depending on the particular story, this ultimate objective may be an explicit accomplishment (to catch the criminal, to escape imprisonment, to win over one's true love) or something more generalized (to find direction in life, to make one's parents proud, to recover from a past trauma). Whatever the case, the Story Goal establishes an unwavering focal point to direct the protagonist's energies. Every act he or she commits is for the purpose of reaching this goal. This is the protagonist's ultimate destination. The light at the end of the tunnel. The most important thing in the world to the protagonist, from the beginning of the story to its end. It must be achieved no matter what.

By matching a Story Problem with a Story Goal, the narrative establishes clear points of beginning and end. The arrival of the Story Problem initiates the plot's journey. Reaching the Story Goal will end it. The remainder of the plot can be envisioned as a string connecting these two events. As long as story action stays on this "line," the narrative will retain its focus and clarity.

## The Path of Action

Yet of course, the Story Goal is not going to fall into the protagonist's lap. Anything worth achieving requires physical effort. This is even more apparent in the dramatically-heightened world of story. The Story Problem imposes a difficult and often complex situation. Overcoming it may be a massive undertaking. The Problem cannot be solved with one simple action, but requires an entire series of actions. To make any progress, the protagonist must organize his or her efforts so he or she may pursue the Goal one step at a time.

The Path of Action makes up the heart of the plot's physical journey. It is the long and difficult road the protagonist must follow to reach the Story Goal. This of course is a figurative road, composed of all actions the protagonist must commit to resolve the story situation. Many tasks must be performed and lesser objectives achieved. With each accomplishment, the protagonist moves closer and closer to his or her final goal. Such goal-oriented actions give the story a sensation of forward progress. This is a necessity in any dramatic narrative. Movement excites interest. Lack of movement loses it. If no one is taking action, the story stands still and boredom overtakes the audience.

However, things can never go exactly as planned. The storyteller must inject doubt into the narrative by creating obstacles to block the protagonist's intended path or setbacks to force the journey in unexpected directions. The protagonist must then find new routes to bypass or overcome these complications, routes that may lead into danger and darkness or force the protagonist to accept challenges he or she would rather not face. Yet no matter how the path may alter, the end destination always remains the same. Despite the twists and turns, the protagonist remains focused upon the Story Goal. He or she must merely find new means to get there.

## *The Source of Main Conflict*

A story is worth little unless it can sustain its audience's attentions from its beginning until its end. To do so, a story must contain an element of *drama.* Drama is created from a state of uncertainty – particularly, uncertainty regarding the outcome of narrative events. Uncertainty causes the audience to ask questions. The audience then continues to pay attention until those questions are answered.

As suggested by the twists and turns of the Path of Action, no narrative journey can ever be easy. The more difficult the journey, the more uncertainty it will hold and therefore the more dramatic it will be. *Conflict* is the chief source of this drama. Something must directly oppose the protagonist's pursuit the Story Goal, turning the journey into a struggle. In the clearest and most unified of narratives, this conflict comes primarily from a single source, known as the *force of antagonism*. Depending upon the story, this opposing force may be another character (known as the antagonist), or may arise from the protagonist's generalized situation or environment. Regardless of the case, this opposing force stands dead-set against the protagonist's actions. Every time the protagonist pushes forward, the force of antagonism pushes back. Opposing forces create conflict. Conflict creates drama. Drama holds the audience's interest out of a desire to know how events will be resolved. This conflict then makes the protagonist's pursuit of the Story Goal all the more meaningful. Because the protagonist must struggle, suffer, and sacrifice for what he or she wants or needs, the victory will be far greater when he or she finally achieves it.

Conflict also has a structural purpose. Conflict creates change. When opposing forces collide, characters must react in ways that change the story's situation. Each outcome then advances the plot in new and unexpected ways. Therefore, a story needs conflict to ensure that its narrative will constantly move forward in the most dramatic fashion.

## The Stakes

So now, the protagonist has a Goal. He or she takes willful action to reach that Goal, only to meet incredible resistance from the Source of the Main Conflict. If this conflict makes the protagonist's journey so difficult, dangerous even, what is to stop the protagonist from deciding the Goal is no longer worth it and giving up? For the story to continue, the protagonist needs a reason to stay in the fight. Enter the Story Spine's final component: The Stakes.

The Stakes are what is "in it" for the protagonist. They are what the protagonist has to gain if he or she succeeds and what the protagonist will lose should he or she fail. Victory has rewards. More importantly, failure has consequences. Sometimes dire consequences. This means the story's outcome holds personal importance to the protagonist. The protagonist feels motivated to continue his or her pursuit out of the desire for reward or the fear of consequence. Thus, the Stakes provide a counter-force that acts to push the protagonist forward in spite of overwhelming conflict. The higher the Stakes, the more conflict the protagonist becomes willing to face. Without sufficient Stakes, the protagonist's actions will seem implausible as there will be no good reason for the protagonist to take on such risk.

Stakes also imbue story events with a greater sense of significance. Stakes explain why characters care. They also explain why the audience should care. When viewers understand the consequences of success or failure, they become emotionally invested in the story's outcome. The audience will want the protagonist to succeed because it knows that terrible things will happen if the protagonist should fail.

The Story Spine must contain all five components to function. Any story will be profoundly weakened if even one component is missing. A story without a Problem lacks purpose. A story without a Goal lacks direction. A story without a clear Path of Action lacks focus. A story without a Source of Main Conflict lacks drama. A story without Stakes lacks significance.

Let us take a look at the Story Spine in action. In *Raiders of the Lost Ark* (1981), the story officially begins when Indiana Jones encounters a Story Problem: He learns the Nazis will soon unearth the Ark of the Covenant, an artifact which will allow them to conquer the world. In reaction, Indy establishes a Story Goal: To find the Ark first and steal it away. To reach this goal, Indy must pursue a Path of Action: First he must persuade his ex-lover Marian to give him an item necessary to locate the Ark. Then he must travel to Egypt and search for the Ark in secret. Then he must escape with the Ark to America. However, a Source of Conflict stands in Indy's way: The Nazis and their allies will stop at nothing to claim the Ark for themselves, including kidnapping and murder. Yet Indy is willing to face these threats due to the Stakes: If Indy succeeds, he will receive the fame and fortune attached to the archaeological find of the century. If Indy fails, the world is doomed to an unstoppable Nazi conquest. These Stakes explain why Indy cares about the outcome and why the audience should care as well. Every element of *Raiders'* plot issues from these five components. *Raiders* contains a clear and effective narrative due to its clear and effective structure.

Compare this to a film of much different character. In *The Godfather* (1972), protagonist Michael Corleone lives a stable and comfortable life until the arrival of a Story Problem: An attack on his father initiates a mafia war against his family. In reaction, Michael establishes a Story Goal: To end the war in a way that will ensure his family's permanent safety. To do this, Michael pursues a Path of Action: First he must kill the man trying to assassinate his father. Then he must escape retribution for this action. Then he must later return to enact a plan that will subdue his family's enemies for good. However, Michael faces a great deal of conflict. Michael must not only deal with his family's enemies, but how the necessary actions run afoul of the law, Michael's personal needs, and his own moral ideals. Yet Michael is willing to take on this conflict seeing that the Stakes are so incredibly high. If Michael succeeds, he will save the lives of his family. If he fails, he and everyone else may perish.

Very short or simple stories can get by with a Story Spine alone. However, as mentioned in the previous chapter, longer forms of storytelling demand additional structure if they wish to maintain the audience's interest for an extended length of time. Because of this, the feature length film further structures its Path of Action into a chain of segments known as STORY SEQUENCES. In each story sequence (typically six to twelve minutes long, depending on the pace of the narrative), the protagonist pursues a distinct sub-objective which the protagonist believes, if achieved, will allow him or her to move one step closer to the ultimate Story Goal. For example, the first half of *Raiders of the Lost Ark* is composed of sequences such as: getting the headpiece from Marian; starting preparations in Cairo; escaping the marketplace; and unearthing the Ark's hiding place. Each sequence presents a distinct sub-adventure that acts to advance the narrative as a whole.

Story sequences begin and end with moments of dramatic change known as TURNING POINTS. A turning point is a significant plot event that brings the action of the previous sequence to an end and launches the action of the next, literally turning the course of the narrative in a new direction. Typically, turning points occur in one of two ways. Either the protagonist achieves his or her sequence objective, allowing him or her to move on to the next stage of the adventure; or an unexpected event forces the protagonist to abandon his or her current course of action in favor of a new and more crucial objective.

Turning points are extremely important to narrative structure and development. They provide the plot's most significant events, placed at strategically-timed intervals that act to reinvigorate story action before the audience's interest has a chance to wane. In addition, turning points allow the narrative to build in intensity as the story progresses. Each turning point adds a complication to the story situation, escalating the level of conflict along with it. Dramatic tension intensifies sequence by sequence, slowly tightening the grip on the audience until the story reaches its climactic resolution.

Screenwriters commonly specialize this structure by organizing story sequences into what are known as ACTS. An act is a group of related story sequences which together constitute a larger movement of plot. Despite the overwhelming emphasis given to it by other writer-analysts, the traditional "3-Act Structure" is really nothing more than a template used to further refine the content and composition of story sequences. This book will not spend much time dwelling upon this misnamed model,\* as it holds little significance to the overarching unified narrative structure to be explained later. However, there is one element of this model that should be mentioned here. Traditionally, the final sequence of each act will end with a turning point bearing far greater dramatic significance than normal. Along with the Inciting Incident, these end-of-act events (labeled the End of 1st Act Turning Point, the Mid-2nd Act Turning Point (or Midpoint), the End of 2nd Act Turning Point, and the Main Story Climax) provide the five most structurally important moments of the story's plot. Along with ending one act and

---

\* Misnamed in that traditional cinematic plot structure is actually composed of four acts of equal length (Act 1, Act 2A, Act 2B, and Act 3). See *Screenwriting Down to the Atoms*, Chapter 6.

beginning the next, each of these "Major Dramatic Turning Points" perform certain special functions that often coincide with the unified narrative structure's most essential developmental events. These important events will be commented upon in later chapters.

## THE PROTAGONIST'S CHARACTER ARC

For a story to be a "story," it must contain characters. In other words, a story must be about human beings (or figurative representations of human beings, as when fantasy or animation grants human behavior to non-human creatures). To put this in yet another way, all stories are about human behaviors – what people do and how they do it. Though this may seem obvious, within this axiom lies a reason storytelling exists. In all cultures, stories are used as tools of social instruction. They teach individuals how to act in what the culture considers a healthy and productive manner. Stories largely do this by showing how characters who behave in proper manners are rewarded, while those who act in improper manners are punished. By illustrating how some actions lead to victory and others to failure, stories encourage their audiences to embrace "correct" attitudes, behaviors, or beliefs while avoiding those deemed "incorrect."

Simple stories such as fables or religious parables do this in a fairly straightforward manner. Characters with established behavioral natures encounter a test. Characters with positive natures pass the test while those with negative natures fail. Such lessons can be strengthened through contrast. At its simplest, this may be done by comparing the fates of two characters with widely-opposing natures (as seen in "The Grasshopper and the Ant" in Chapter 1-2). Yet while such stories may allow the audience to recognize what behaviors are considered correct or incorrect, they fulfill only half of storytelling's sociological purpose. These stories feature one-dimensional caricatures with innate natures that cannot be changed and therefore provide the audience with no instruction regarding how they might change their own behaviors so they too may receive reward or avoid punishment. A story is far more sociologically potent when the receiver can apply its lesson directly to his or her own life. More sophisticated stories accomplish this goal by presenting the audience with a character who undergoes a process of personal growth or change. Through this change, the audience not only sees the consequences of two contrasting sets of behaviors, but observes a logical path by which an individual may potentially evolve for the better or the worse.

A character begins the story with one set of attitudes, behaviors, or beliefs. When the character encounters the story's test, events affect the character emotionally and psychologically, causing those attitudes, behaviors, or beliefs to change. Essentially, the character starts as one type of person and finishes as another. As a result of this change, the character's situation either improves or worsens. If the situation improves for the character, the audience must conclude that the new behaviors are more beneficial and should be personally adopted. If the situation worsens, the audience must conclude that the new behaviors are harmful and should be avoided.

The cinematic story presents this process of change through a structure called the CHARACTER ARC. On its surface, the Character Arc is fairly simple. The protagonist begins the story with a preexisting mindset of personal attitudes, values, and beliefs which decide how he or she thinks and behaves. There are positive aspects to this mindset as well as negative. When confronted by story events, the protagonist uses this mindset to decide how to react. Sometimes these reactions help the protagonist, but far more often negative attitudes and behaviors cause the protagonist to make improper decisions, leading to struggle and failure. A sensible protagonist eventually realizes these attitudes or behaviors are ill-equipped to deal with the story situation and resolves him or herself to a course of personal change. If the protagonist commits to the proper change, this transformation allows the character to succeed. Yet not all protagonists possess such wisdom. Some refuse to change or change in the wrong manner. These protagonists remain unable to effectively deal with the story's problems and will ultimately fail.

While simple in theory, the cinematic Character Arc must be a bit more complicated in practice. This is chiefly because feature films must present worlds that pass for reality. Essential to this reality is the accurate portrayal of human behavior. Contrary to what the previous paragraph may suggest, real-life personal change is neither simple nor easy. Human beings are not like computer programs, coldly analyzing their current situations and then registering the most logically-viable solution. If this were so, few of us would have any problems in life. In truth, we humans are frequently irrational when it comes to our behavior, particularly in the way we tend to ignore or defend our personal faults. Most of us would like to believe we are perfectly fine the way we are, even when clear evidence exists to the contrary. When people do recognize their flaws, many are highly reluctant to do anything about them. Personal change is hard. It is inconvenient. It is frightening. Given the choice, most of us are satisfied to say, "This is just who I am. I can't do anything about it. The world should just accept it."

Human nature tends to be self-defeating. Though we all would like to be better people, have healthier relationships, or find greater success, there is always some irrational impulse that pushes us in the opposite direction. We are often selfish when we know we should be generous, rude when we should be friendly, lazy when we know we should be disciplined. We say unkind things to people we love. We hold back in fear in moments that require action. We often see the high road but instead choose the path of least resistance. It is as if we are all split into two selves; the strong, capable, and virtuous individual we know we should be; and the weak, flawed, and selfish person we too frequently are. Within each of us rages a war of conflicting impulses; a war that our flawed self too often wins.

The cinematic Character Arc portrays accurate human behavior by illustrating this same war within the protagonist. Like the Story Spine, the Character Arc develops by way of a conflict between two opposing sides. Yet while the Story Spine presents a physical battle, the conflict of the Character Arc is largely psychological. Two opposing forces lie within the protagonist's mind: an INTERNAL NEED motivating the protagonist to become a better and more capable individual, and a FATAL FLAW standing in the way.

The protagonist begins the story as an emotionally or psychologically incomplete individual. There is a certain lack within the character's existence that prevents him or her from becoming as successful or emotionally-satisfied as he or she might possibly be. The character may need the love and acceptance of others. The character may need to forgive him or herself for past wrongs. The character may need a feeling of worth or accomplishment. Or possibly, the character simply needs to accept what he or she cannot control. Whatever the case, this lack aches to be fulfilled. This is the character's Internal Need. Sometimes the character is aware of this need. More often, he or she is not. Yet still, the Internal Need calls out to the character. It motivates the character to take action. However, to achieve this Need, the character must change the ways he or she thinks or behaves. Until this happens, the character will remain unhappy, unfulfilled, and incomplete.

Unfortunately, the path to the Internal Need has been blocked. Not by forces external to the character (though the character may blame all of life's problems on other people or things), but by a psychological barrier of the protagonist's own making. This barrier is known as the Fatal Flaw. Contrary to what many assume, the Fatal Flaw does not refer to a single negative quality or personality trait, but rather the *false mental paradigm* from which all the character's negative behaviors arise. To borrow a concept from psychology, "paradigms" are the mental structures we construct to evaluate the world around us. Past experiences provide collections of attitudes, ideas, and beliefs from which we develop an elaborate mindset to act as the "lens" through which we view our reality, interpret events, and assign meanings. Paradigms present the "truth" of the world seen through the eyes of a single individual. However, truth is in the eye of the beholder. Each individual has had different life experiences, and therefore possesses a paradigm unique from any other. Differences in paradigms often cause interpersonal conflict. One person's perception of "truth" does not match another person's, and no amount of arguing will persuade either party that he or she is wrong. Furthermore, a paradigm may not be in any way accurate or true. A misevaluation of past events may lead a person to adopt falsehoods into his or her conception of self, the world, or others. If these beliefs go uncorrected, the individual may develop an entirely warped view of reality. This often leads to harmful or self-destructive behaviors. False paradigms can cause hatred or prejudice. Phobias or anxieties. Depression or low self-esteem.

Even criminality or mental illness. By following false beliefs, individuals ultimately do themselves harm. Yet from the warped perspective of the flawed individual, he or she has done nothing wrong. It is the world that is at fault, not him or herself.

Likewise in story, past experiences (or in some cases, a lack thereof) have misled the protagonist to develop certain inaccurate, self-limiting, and often self-destructive beliefs that cause the protagonist to view him or herself, other people, or the world in an incorrect light. What the character believes to be true is in fact untrue. This mismatch between belief and reality causes friction. Negative traits inevitably arise that cause the character to struggle with life and create unnecessary conflict with others. To provide a few examples, in *Casablanca,* Rick's heartbreak at the hands of Ilsa has caused him to conclude that caring for other people will only get him hurt. This paradigm has left Rick cold, and emotionally isolated. He now refuses to take any risk for another person's sake out of the certainty that he will eventually regret it. In *Rocky,* the title character's past failures to gain the love and support of others has led him to believe he is nothing but a loser. Because of this self-perception, Rocky has grown bitter and resentful, submissive and socially-awkward. In *Star Wars,* Luke's lack of life experience has left him a wide-eyed fool with no more sense or wisdom than that of a child. From his paradigm of ignorance, Luke never seems to know the correct way to react to the situations he encounters, acting fearful and reluctant at some times, foolish and impetuous at others.

These traits hold characters back in life. Any opportunity to achieve a happier, more productive existence ends up sabotaged by counter-productive behaviors. As long as a character maintains his or her flawed perceptions, he or she is doomed to constantly fail. The character will continue to pursue life in the wrong way, causing more problems and keeping the Internal Need forever out of reach.

Fortunately, false paradigms can be cured. In real life, this can be done through psychotherapy. A psychotherapist seeks out a patient's inaccurate beliefs, encourages the patient to challenge those beliefs, and then ultimately replaces them with a more productive view of reality. The cinematic

Character Arc causes the protagonist to undergo a similar process, albeit by far harsher methods. While psychotherapy encourages a slow and gradual change through self-reflection, the Character Arc forces rapid change through a trial by fire. Its primary tool of this trial is dramatic conflict.

As the protagonist encounters the Story Problem and pursues objectives along the Path of Action, he or she encounters obstacles and opposition. Because of the protagonist's fatally-flawed perspective, he or she evaluates the situation with faulty thinking and chooses to deal with these problems by incorrect or ineffective methods. These flawed methods lead to setbacks and failures. The longer the protagonist presses on in this manner, the more mistakes accumulate. Through such events, the Fatal Flaw is exposed to the light of day. Until now, the protagonist may have never realized his or her attitudes or behaviors were a problem. Yet in the face of these mounting setbacks and failures, the character's inadequacies become obvious.

Now that the Fatal Flaw has been exposed, the protagonist must be motivated to challenge its underlying beliefs. The unwanted outcomes of the protagonist's flawed behaviors eventually lead him or her to a moment of CRUCIAL DECISION. Faced with the ways his or her actions have inadvertently worsened the story situation, the protagonist can do one of to things. The first is to deny the problem. Some protagonists refuse to acknowledge their need for change and instead cling to their flawed beliefs. These protagonists then intensify their negative behaviors out of the belief that they can overcome the story's problems through sheer brute force. This of course is the wrong road. By entrenching themselves deeper into their Fatal Flaws, these protagonists commit actions that make their situations worse and worse, ultimately leading to their final defeat. The second path is a harder road, yet one that will ultimately lead to salvation. Faced with the moment of Crucial Decision, more sensible protagonists take a step back and reevaluate the past actions that put them into their current predicament. Since previous actions have only worsened the situation, the protagonist must conclude that he or she is doing something wrong. A road to victory cannot be found by sticking to the same old methods. If the protagonist is to overcome the story's obstacles, he or she must identify where he or she has gone wrong and find new and better means to reach the Story Goal. In other words, the protagonist challenges his or her past thoughts and actions, finds them lacking, and out of necessity chooses to replace them with attitudes and behaviors that appear better-suited to deal with the story's problems.

Now that the protagonist is open to personal change, he or she must be convinced of the falsity of his or her mental paradigm. Once this occurs, the false paradigm can be abandoned and replaced with one far more beneficial and truer to reality. The story's dramatic conflict has forced the protagonist to experiment with new attitudes and behaviors. To the protagonist's surprise, these new attitudes and behaviors succeed where the old ones failed. With this, the protagonist finally sees the light. Until now, he or she has been stumbling about in life, doing everything in the wrong way. But now, events have disproved the character's old beliefs. As the old paradigm starts to crumble, the protagonist receives a more accurate view of reality and now sees how he or she must change to find happiness or success. The protagonist is then reborn as a new person, one with the wisdom and strength of will to do what is necessary to not only defeat the story conflict, but traverse the barriers that stand in the way of the Internal Need. By challenging and then abandoning his or her flawed mental paradigm, the protagonist transforms into a more capable individual, one no longer plagued by counter-productive behaviors or misheld beliefs.

As we can see, story conflict does more than present the character with a test. It also acts as the main motivator for personal change. While the protagonist's Internal Need may ache to be fulfilled, this is not enough to initiate his or her transformation. True to human nature, the protagonist begins the story a victim to inertia. The protagonist does not want to change. The protagonist fears change. He or she is not yet willing to risk the effort or commit the sacrifices necessary to become a better or more capable person. Story conflict counters this by imposing an imminent threat that demands the protagonist improve him or herself as quickly as possible. Whether the protagonist wants to change is irrelevant. The protagonist *must* change or else he or she will meet an undesirable fate.

Those protagonists who refuse transformation have no one to blame for their failures but themselves. The protagonist could have changed for the better, but chose not to. Through defeat, stories communicate a different kind of message. Rather than reward those who improve themselves, these stories punish those who refuse to abandon their flawed ways. As such, the story acts as a warning. If one acts in the same way as the character, he or she will be punished in life as well.

As we can see, the basic premise of the Character Arc is fairly Darwinean in nature. The character must either evolve for the better or perish. However, just like in Darwin's model of evolution, the protagonist will not find success by just any change. It must be the correct change. The protagonist must adopt the one behavioral value that will make him or her best-suited for survival in his or her particular story world. But what is this one value? What exact change must the protagonist make to achieve victory? Furthermore, why is this one value so important? The answers to these questions are found in the third dimension of storytelling: the theme.

## THE THEMATIC ARGUMENT

Theme is an abstract concept by nature, and thus has always been difficult to define or comprehend. As stated in the previous chapter, the theme is what the story "believes in." It contains the underlying values, principles, or beliefs the story intends to express. A clear and recognizable theme will guide the choice of story content, deciding what kind of actions and events are relevant to the story's message and which are not. In this way, the theme provides cohesion. It ensures that every narrative element revolves around a single set of ideas and works to express a clear and unified meaning.

The fact that theme is abstract and invisible poses a number of difficulties. Since the cinema can only communicate through what can be seen or heard, the theme cannot be delivered directly. One cannot put on screen that which has no shape or form. For communication to occur, the theme's abstract ideas must be translated into observable characters or events. But whenever there is translation, there is always the risk of mistranslation. The storyteller may fail to communicate his or her message clearly enough for the audience to understand. The audience may then misinterpret content and assign meanings the storyteller did not intend. Sometimes storytellers over-compensate for this possibility by expressing thematic content overtly, often with an over-reliance on dialogue and heavy-handed symbolism. However, thematic material can distract from the story when delivered in this manner. What should be a story turns into a sermon. What should be entertainment turns into propaganda. To avoid this problem, it is important to make the distinction between a thematic message delivered *through* a story opposed to one merely delivered *by* a story, as the former is far more effective than the latter.

When thematic content is communicated *by* a story, this means ideological material has been tacked on to an existing narrative like superficial orna-mentation. A piece of dialogue here, a symbolic visual there, a rousing speech with an upswell of music to make it perfectly clear that this is the moment when the audience is supposed to learn something. Since the story could have gotten along perfectly well without these additions, this content is extraneous to the narrative and stands out in an unnatural light. The storyteller is attempting to impose meaning through outside interference rather than allowing the story to express itself through the natural dramatic process.

In contrast, when theme is delivered *through* a story, the thematic message is derived from the content of the narrative itself. In a great story, plot and character material pull a double duty. As introduced in Chapter 1-2 with "The Grasshopper and the Ant," narrative elements act as representatives of ideological meaning. Thematic content is not separate from plot and character. They are actually one and the same. In this way, the theme develops invisibly under the cover of the film's observable action. By paying atten-tion to plot and character, the audience simultaneously receives the story's meaning.

This process of thematic communication is often difficult for developing writers to understand. Fortunately, a basic narrative structure exists to aid this process, one that naturally integrates into the established structures of character and plot. This structure is called the THEMATIC ARGUMENT.

There is a common misconception (particularly among beginners) that the expression of theme remains stable and absolute from the beginning of a story to its end. Many assume the theme must be chiseled into stone from the start and then repetitively hammered into the audience's heads without change or alteration. Yet in the best of cinematic narratives, this could not be further from the truth. Like plot and character, a story's theme develops over the course of the narrative through a process of *dramatic change*. At the beginning, the story's premise establishes certain values, principles, or ideas to be examined by the story's events. As the narrative develops through plot and character, dramatic conflict creates questions and doubts regarding the worth or veracity of these thematic ideals. Since the story's dramatic outcome remains uncertain, the thematic message remains uncertain as well. This state of ideological doubt persists until the final climax. It is only once all dramatic conflicts have been resolved that the story can finally express its meaning in a clear and conclusive fashion.

Like the structures of plot and character, the Thematic Argument develops by way of a conflict between two opposing sides. While the Story Spine presents an external conflict between two physical forces, and the Character Arc an internal conflict between two psychological forces, the Thematic Argument contains an ideological conflict between two diametrically opposed values, ideas, or beliefs. We call this structure the Thematic Argument because this is exactly what it provides. It is an argument, a debate, a battle between two contradictory principles. On one side of the battle is the specific value, idea, or belief the story wishes to promote. We will label this the THEME. On the other side is the exact opposite of this value, idea, or belief. We will call this the ANTI-THEME. A theme of courage is opposed by an anti-theme of fear. A theme of confidence is opposed by an anti-theme of self-doubt. A theme of honesty is opposed by dishonesty. In this way, Thematic Arguments can be expressed as simple ideological dualities: COURAGE vs. FEAR, CONFIDENCE vs. SELF-DOUBT, HONESTY vs. DISHONESTY. These two sides engage in a debate through the story's physical actions to decide which is better, which is stronger, which leads to victory and which to defeat.

To provide the strongest argument in favor of the story's intended theme, content related to the opposing anti-theme must be granted equal presence within the narrative. Anyone with experience in competitive debate should understand why this is. In debate, it is not enough to simply provide evidence in support of one's own position. One must also recognize and then disprove the arguments of the opposing side. An idea is proven superior only if it can defeat those levied against it. For a proper and balanced Thematic Argument, a story must present its theme and anti-theme in equal amount. A story about telling the truth must be filled with characters who lie. A story about justice must contain plenty of injustice. A story about freedom must show what it is like to have freedoms taken away. Through narrative action, the story puts both values to the test, allowing the audience to see the positive and negative outcomes of each. Eventually, the behaviors on one side of the argument conquer those on the other side, winning the ideological debate.

Now comes the tricky part. We are not creating a sermon, a lecture, or an essay on morals. We are creating a story. Stories are meant to entertain. The cinematic story primarily entertains through conflicts of plot and character. If the Thematic Argument is to deliver its message without distracting from the entertainment, its ideological debate must not occur separately from these conflicts. It instead must develop through these conflicts themselves. Basically, theme uses the conflicts of plot and character as a Trojan Horse. The storyteller imbues characters and situations with certain qualities which allow them to act as symbolic representatives of the theme or anti-theme. When forces collide, one side symbolically fights for the story's thematic value and the other side for the anti-thematic value. This way, the story entertains while it communicates and communicates while it entertains. The Thematic Argument not only avoids distracting from the entertainment, but *is* the entertainment itself.

To use an imaginative metaphor, think of the Thematic Argument as a war between an angel and a demon. Both the angel (the theme) and the demon (the anti-theme) wish to destroy each other. However, both entities are abstract beings lacking physical bodies. This means there is no way for the angel and demon to fight each other directly. The only solution is for both parties to *possess the bodies* of mortal men or women so they may take action through them. Metaphorically speaking, the theme and anti-theme possess the bodies of characters in order to force them to do their bidding. If a story has a theme of justice and an anti-theme of injustice, some characters will be metaphorically possessed by the spirit of injustice. Due to this possession, these characters are compelled to act in an unjust manner. Because they play for injustice's "team," every win by these characters will also be a win for the anti-theme. At the same time, other characters are metaphorically possessed by the spirit of justice. These characters feel driven to fight for justice's ideals. Aligned on justice's team, every victory for these characters will also be a victory for the thematic value. In this way, characters take an active part in the Thematic Argument without their knowledge. This turns an ideological battle into a physical one. The ethical or moral debate is given substance through conflicting characters.

To summarize, while the two sides of a story's dramatic conflict are engaged in a physical battle, they are also simultaneously engaged in an ideological battle. Each side of the conflict champions not only their own causes, but also the cause of the theme or anti-theme. Because of this, the outcome of the story's physical conflict also decides the winner of the Thematic Argument. When the two opposing sides meet at the story's final climax, the champion of one value defeats the champion of the other value, proving it to be the greater of the two sides.

In the best of stories, theme and anti-theme permeate plot action like water in a sponge. Every event reflects some aspect of either the theme or anti-theme. Every conflict illustrates what can happen when theme and anti-theme collide. Content irrelevant to the Thematic Argument should be avoided whenever possible, as this dilutes ideological focus. When executed properly, every win or loss will not only advance the plot, but make an argument for or against the theme or anti-theme. As both sides of the dramatic conflict take stronger and stronger actions, the theme and anti-theme make stronger and stronger arguments through them. This culminates at the main story climax when one side wins and the other is defeated, wrapping up both the Story Spine and the Thematic Argument in a single event.

The omnipresence of theme and anti-theme should also extend to a story's cast of characters. When best executed, the attitudes and behaviors of every character will somehow embody an aspect of either the theme or anti-theme. At their extremes, a character may be a "white knight" (the purest embodiment of the theme) or a "black hat" (the purest embodiment of the anti-theme).* The remainder of the cast exists somewhere between the two extremes within a wide spectrum of attitudes and behaviors that express the theme or anti-theme in various degrees and intensities. Split into two opposing camps, the cast is not unlike the two sides in a game of chess. One side is light and the other is dark. Some pieces are strong while others are weak. Together, they take part in the moves and counter-moves of a grand ideological battle. This dichotomy does more than provide the story with thematic clarity. It also allows ample opportunities to explore the theme and anti-theme in a variety of contexts and situations. With a wide range of character personalities, the story is able to demonstrate the many ways the theme and anti-theme can manifest in human behavior. Any time characters come into conflict, we see how those characters' particular embodiments of theme or anti-theme fare against one another.

*Star Wars* provides a clear example, as the film weaves its thematic dichotomy right into its premise. In *Star Wars*, all characters are aligned on either the "Light Side of the Force" or the "Dark Side." The religion of the Jedi teaches that all living beings are connected by an energy called the Force. Those on the Light Side believe it is their duty to use the power of the Force to protect and preserve all living things. Those on the Dark Side abuse the Force's power for selfish gain. This division establishes the story's theme and anti-theme. The story pits characters who take selfless actions for the good of others against those who harm and oppress others for personal gain. This can be further generalized as a duality between ALTRUISM and ANTI-ALTRUISM.†

---

*Although these character types are certainly not mandatory in every story.

† Unfortunately, the English language lacks an exact antonym to altruism. Altruism is defined as the selfless concern for the welfare of others. Its opposite would be (at its most conservative) the disregard of others to serve oneself, or (at its worst) the intentional harm of others for personal gain. An equally adequate term may be the portmanteau "maltruism."

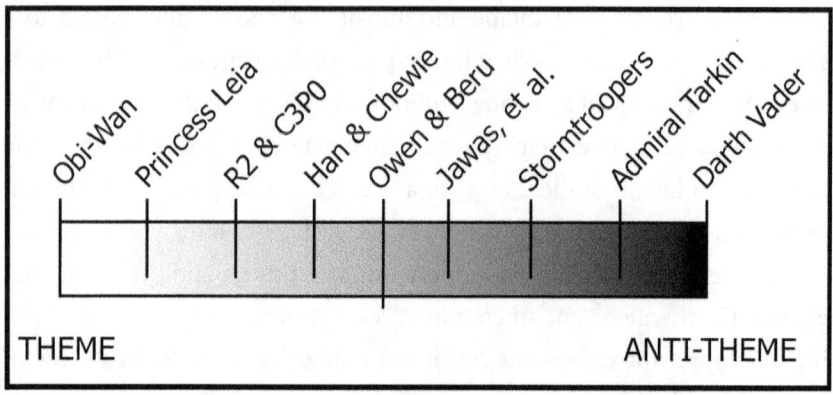

The purest embodiment of the theme is found in Obi-Wan Kenobi (the white knight). The strongest representative of the anti-theme is Darth Vader (the black hat). Between Obi-Wan and Darth Vader stretches a linear spectrum of characters with behaviors that range from those highly thematic to those highly anti-thematic with a neutral gray area in between. First along the "light" side of the spectrum we find Princess Leia. Leia is second only to Obi-Wan in her dedication to the thematic value. However, her motives are not as pure. As a Jedi, Obi-Wan serves the thematic value as a holy ideal. Leia on the other hand is a diplomat and statesperson, and is motivated by political concerns. She does not believe in the Force, yet nevertheless serves its ideals out of her personal ethics. Less strongly aligned are the droids R2D2 and C3P0. The droids also serve the thematic value, but based on the weaker motives of loyalty and duty. The mercenaries Han Solo and Chewbacca reside on the far cusp of the thematic scale. Han and Chewie are willing to serve the thematic value, but for the far more degraded motives of personal gain. These two eventually become heroic by shifting their behavior closer to the lighter side of the spectrum.

In the middle of the gray area between theme and anti-theme we find Uncle Owen and Aunt Beru. These two may have once believed in the thematic value, but now act only to ensure their own survival. This neutrality puts them in the cross-fire between the theme and anti-theme, costing them their lives.

Moving into the anti-thematic side of the spectrum, we find that each thematic character has his or her own anti-thematic counterpart. First along this end of the scale are the Jawas, the Sand People, and the scum of Mos Eisley. Like Han Solo and Chewbacca, these creatures look out for their own interests, but unlike Han and Chewie, their behaviors are more anti-thematic in nature. They will not hesitate to cheat or harm others for personal gain. The droids have their opposite in the Stormtroopers. Like the droids, the Stormtroopers act out of duty. Yet they do so for the principles of the anti-theme. Darker still is Leia's counterpart Admiral Tarkin. Like Leia, Tarkin is motivated by political aims. However, these aims are highly anti-thematic in nature, using tyranny and oppression to promote the black-hearted ambitions of the Empire. Darkest of all is Darth Vader. Vader represents the anti-theme in its purest form in that he spreads tyranny and oppression purely for his own power and glory. The thematic value of altruism is repulsive to him and he is willing to crush anyone who serves it.

It should be noted that the protagonist Luke Skywalker is not included in this list. This is because the protagonist is typically not aligned with either the theme or the anti-theme when the story begins. Instead, the protagonist starts as an independent player yet to choose a side. However, the forces of story conflict prevent the protagonist from staying neutral forever. To return to our earlier metaphor, it is as if the angel of theme and the demon of anti-theme both recognize the protagonist as the story's most important player and thus compete for the possession of his or her soul. As the protagonist encounters story events and interacts with variously-aligned characters, the protagonist's attitudes and beliefs are subject to an ideological tug-of-war. Representatives of both theme and anti-theme attempt to persuade the protagonist to join their side. At the same time, events and their outcomes provide the protagonist with evidence in favor of one side of the argument or the other. This pressure progressively intensifies until the protagonist finally chooses a side.

With this decision, the protagonist willfully takes on the role of the chosen value's champion. The protagonist imbues his or her actions with the qualities of the theme or anti-theme, and from that point onward fights for its cause. In *Star Wars,* this moment occurs just after the story's Midpoint when Luke and his comrades find themselves trapped aboard the Death

Star. Separated from Obi-Wan, Luke decides to take it upon himself to rescue Princess Leia. With this, Luke finally chooses to forego his former passivity and indecision and dedicates himself in service of the thematic ideal. Luke becomes a champion of heroic altruism. His actions are empowered by this decision and henceforth fights not only for his own cause, but for that of a greater ideological ideal.

It is in this choice that we see a connection exists not only between the Thematic Argument and the Story Spine, but also between the Thematic Argument and the protagonist's Character Arc. The protagonist's Internal Need and Fatal Flaw are directly related to the theme and anti-theme. The Internal Need motivates the protagonist to change his or her behavior in ways closer aligned to the thematic value. The Fatal Flaw resists this change, urging the protagonist to maintain attitudes and behaviors anti-thematic in nature. When the protagonist encounters his or her Crucial Decision, the protagonist is essentially presented with a choice between the theme and the anti-theme. If the protagonist abandons the Fatal Flaw in favor of change, he or she is in fact embracing the theme. If the protagonist rejects personal change in favor of the Fatal Flaw, he or she chooses to side with the anti-theme. Therefore, the protagonist's Crucial Decision also represents his or her choice in terms of thematic alignment. (More on this will be covered in later chapters.)

However, just because the protagonist chooses a side, this does not necessarily mean that side will win. What the protagonist believes to be the right choice does not always prove to be the correct path to victory. In *Chinatown*, Jake Gittes chooses integrity over corruption, yet this side meets failure in the story's end. In *Braveheart*, William Wallace's choice also leads to failure. Why is this sometimes the case? What is the purpose of a hero who meets defeat?

The Thematic Argument uses dramatic conflict to prove whether values, attitudes, or beliefs are correct or incorrect. To put things simply, the Thematic Argument uses a story as a laboratory test to show how certain social values or beliefs fare within hypothetical situations. The Thematic Argument delivers its conclusive statement on that value or belief by way of a two-part structure. First, it dramatizes a choice between two opposing values. Then, it demonstrates whether that choice leads to victory or failure. If the protagonist succeeds by way of the chosen value, that value is proven "correct." If the value leads the protagonist to failure, that value is disproved in favor of its opposite.

As we can see, the ultimate expression of the Thematic Argument is dependent upon the two key moments of the Character Arc and Story Spine, namely the Crucial Decision and the plot's final climax. Hence, a story's final message can only be fully communicated by the combined outcomes of the Story Spine, Character Arc, and Thematic Argument. As this relates to the interaction between narrative structures, this process will be explained further in the next two chapters. However, it would be wise to take heed of this two-part structure now. As we shall see later, this combination of structural events becomes the key to understanding not only the communication of theme, but the entire unified structure upon which all traditional cinematic storytelling is built.

Before concluding, I must warn that while the Thematic Argument communicates meaning, it does not in and of itself communicate TOTAL MEANING. The Thematic Argument, while important, provides only a single contribution to the story's total message. Broadly speaking, the theme and anti-theme exist to give the story's physical content a unified ideological focus. They ensure that a story's events revolve around a single pair of opposing values. However, as you may have noticed, these opposing values tend to be fairly broad in definition. Simple dualities such as Honesty vs. Dishonesty, Individualism vs. Conformity, or Justice vs. Injustice leave plenty of room for interpretation. Honesty, individualism, and justice can all be dramatized in many different ways and may lead to many different outcomes. The same can be said for dishonesty, conformity, and injustice. While this gives the Thematic Argument great flexibility, the implied social, moral, or ethical message remains far too broad to provide any real ideological impact. A message of "honesty=good, dishonesty=bad" is far too simplistic and does not take into account the many vagaries, dilemmas, and moral contradictions which surround issues encountered in daily life.

In comparison, the *total meaning* of a cinematic story is far more exact. It is derived not from one, but a sum of multiple factors existing deeper within the narrative text. The battle between theme and anti-theme provides a key contribution to this greater message, but cannot express it on its own. Since these additional factors are quite complicated and require advanced analysis, their discussion has been reserved for Part II of this book.

As for now, we will remain focused on narrative structure. We have identified the cinematic story's three basic narrative structures. Now we must find the means by which they fit together. As we shall see, the Story Spine, Character Arc, and Thematic Argument do not operate in isolation, but live and thrive in close cooperation. The experience we know as a great cinematic story comes not from an individual structure, or even the sum of its three individual structures, but what happens when those structures interact.

# CHAPTER 1-4

# BASIC INTERACTIONS

To summarize previous chapters, though it may be possible to separate the cinematic story's three primary structures for independent analysis, these structures certainly do not operate in isolation within the course of the narrative. Nothing is isolated in the cinematic narrative. Everything is connected to everything else. The Story Spine, Character Arc, and Thematic Argument are not three sets of track running in parallel under their own power and volition. Instead, they are intertwined in symbiotic relationships where each is dependent upon the others for growth and development. In this way, the three basic structures move together as one.

This chapter explores the basic means by which these structures interact. We begin with the relationship between the Story Spine and the Character Arc. Then we will examine how this relationship allows the Thematic Argument to deliver its ultimate meaning.

## STORY SPINE & CHARACTER ARC

Most beginners approach screencraft under the belief that plot is the primary and most important element of storytelling. However, this impression exists only because plot is the most visible element. A closer look at the Story Spine shows that plot, on its most basic level, is not designed to revolve around its own content, but the wants, needs, fears, and limitations of characters—specifically, those of the protagonist. After all, the Story Spine is not composed of just any Story Problem or Story Goal, or so on. It is made up of the specific problem the *protagonist* faces, the ultimate goal set by the *protagonist,* the path of actions the *protagonist* takes, the conflict opposing the *protagonist,* and the *protagonist's* personal stakes.* The protagonist stands at the center of the plot's universe. Every structural event pertains to a single character and the issues he or she must face. This means the plot is personal, to a single human being. Since all plot events issue from the Story Spine, and the Story Spine is oriented around its protagonist, it must be concluded that all plot originates from that character and his or her personal problems, goals, wants, and needs.

Though this may seem to be a simple and obvious truth, it stands in stark opposition to the way screenwriting is frequently approached. Many poor scripts treat the protagonist as little more than a warm body who exists for no purpose other than to carry out story events. Sole focus is given to the mechanizations of plot, turning the protagonist into a cog whose only function is to move things from Point A to Point B. Such scripts create a hollow and unsatisfying experience. This is simply because they create empty worlds with no one to revolve around. In a good story, character is the source of plot. Dramatic action issues from the protagonist's personal wants and needs. By neglecting their protagonists, poor stories get this backwards. Plot attempts to move character instead of the character moving the plot.

To make matters worse, stories that neglect their protagonists also neglect the needs of their audience. The protagonist acts as the audience's emotional surrogate. The audience experiences story events by viewing them through the protagonist's eyes. Without a strong surrogate, the audience has no one through whom they can experience emotion or meaning. In such an impersonal story, the plot becomes nothing but "stuff happening." Events

---

* Because of this, the Story Spine can be alternatively labeled the Protagonist's Spine. This sets it apart from the fact that supporting characters possess their own personal spines which act to motivate their behaviors as well. See *Screenwriting Down to the Atoms*, Chapter 7 (or *Absolute Essentials* Chapter 4).

may occur, but without the wants, needs, fears, and limitations of a character to give those events context and meaning, the audience will find little reason to care. An impersonal story experience is an unsatisfying experience. If a story wishes to engage its audience emotionally as well as intellectually, plot must be orientated around character. Not the other way around.

But what exactly does this mean? How does the dimension of plot orientate itself around the needs of character? As related in the previous chapter, the cinematic Character Arc dramatizes a process of change within the protagonist. If the protagonist changes in the proper manner, he or she is rewarded. If the protagonist refuses to change or changes in an improper manner, he or she is punished. In other words, a story revolves around the concept of personal growth. The Story Spine serves the Character Arc by constructing a physical *arena* filled with threats and obstacles intentionally designed to force this growth to occur. I refer to the plot as an arena in the same sense as a gladiatorial arena. In a gladiatorial arena, a combatant enters a situation in which he or she must overcome certain obstacles and challenges before he or she is allowed to leave. A plot does the same thing, only its obstacles and challenges have been designed so that it is impossible for the protagonist to succeed unless he or she first commits to the proper personal change. The physical conflicts found in the plot create a situation in which personal change becomes both logical and necessary. So, if the protagonist wishes to succeed, he or she *must* change in the required manner. There is no other option.

To expand further upon this, it can be said that the Story Problem and Story Goal, as important as they are to any worthwhile story, are really nothing more than EXCUSES invented by the storyteller for the purpose of motivating personal change. The Problem and Goal create a situation that forces the protagonist to get off his or her butt, take action, encounter resistance to the Fatal Flaw, and from lessons learned, grow as an individual. Developing screenwriters are often led to believe that the Character Arc is of secondary importance to the plot. Too many have the impression that the Arc is merely some additional ingredient thrown into the mix to spice up events. However, this could not be further from the truth. Regardless of what conflicts may exist within the plot, the entirety of the physical narrative revolves around the issue of personal change. All events exist to motivate the protagonist to change the way he or she thinks and behaves. The Crucial Decision then becomes the story's pivotal moment. Once the protagonist chooses to accept or reject personal change, the remainder of the narrative shows the outcomes of this decision. From this perspective, it becomes clear that the structure of plot is in fact completely subservient to the structure of character. The plot's physical events have only two real purposes: to motivate the protagonist to make personal decisions, and to then reveal the positive or negative outcomes of those decisions. The Character Arc is the true center of a great cinematic narrative. The Story Spine merely orchestrates the protagonist's transformation.

To visualize how this works, it helps to imagine the storyteller as the "god" of the story's world. Like the Olympian gods of ancient myth, the storyteller has the ability to manipulate the protagonist's environment in order to throw him or her into difficult or dangerous situations. The storyteller-god does not do this for fun, but out of pity. When the story begins, the storyteller-god recognizes the protagonist as a flawed, incomplete human being. The storyteller-god wishes the protagonist to find his or her Internal Need so the character may become a more successful or satisfied individual. Unfortunately, the protagonist is presently unable or unwilling to attain this Need due to a deep-seeded Fatal Flaw. The only way for the storyteller-god to dislodge the protagonist from this unsatisfactory rut of existence and put him or her on a road to personal change is by throwing chaos into the protagonist's life. The storyteller-god devises a Story Problem, one which turns the protagonist's life upside-down and demands immediate action.

Forced into action by the Story Problem, the protagonist finds him or herself caught up in an adventure. But this is not just any adventure. The storyteller-god has devised a fiendish scenario filled with problems impossible to overcome unless the protagonist first confronts and abandons his or her Fatal Flaw. In other words, story conflicts have been tailor-designed to challenge the protagonist's specific faults and force him or her to commit to the proper change. Thus, the story intends to benefit the protagonist through a trial by fire. Its conflicts purge the protagonist of his or her flawed attitudes and behaviors so he or she may grow into a stronger and wiser individual capable of attaining the Internal Need. In summary, the storyteller-god challenges the protagonist with a Story Problem. A Story Goal provides a potential solution. Yet the only way for the protagonist to reach that solution is to undergo a process of personal change. The storyteller-god transforms the character by manipulating the character's world.

Yet of course some protagonists fail the test created by the storyteller-god. Rather than recognize the need for personal change, these protagonists cling even tighter to their Fatal Flaws out of stubbornness, selfishness, ignorance, or fear. By refusing to change, these characters defy the wishes of the storyteller-god and therefore must be punished. The storyteller-god devised the story's test to ultimately do good for the protagonist. It was intended to lead the protagonist to a better and more satisfying existence. Yet by rejecting this path, the protagonist also rejects this gift. In response, the storyteller-god turns its back on the protagonist and allows the story to defeat him or her.

Let us see how this works in action. In *The Matrix*, Neo is a man of great potential, yet he lives a dull, insignificant life due to a flawed belief in his own insignificance. Neo must abandon this belief or else he will never reach his true greatness. To force this to occur, the storyteller-god throws Neo into an extreme situation. Neo suddenly finds himself burdened with the role of humanity's potential savior. Neo did not choose this burden. The story forced it upon him. Nevertheless, Neo is now stuck in an adventure he must see through to the end or else he will face dire consequences. Yet Neo resists at first. This new role requires that he abandon his old beliefs, something Neo fears to do. To counter this, the storyteller-god throws challenges and obstacles in Neo's way that have been intentionally designed to force Neo to grow and change. Eventually, this manipulation of plot presents Neo with a dilemma whereby he must either fully commit to the proper change or meet irrevocable defeat. By choosing to change, Neo passes the story's test, leading him not only to victory, but to his Internal Need in the process.

As seen in *The Matrix,* the most extreme of situations are often necessary to force the protagonist to change. After all, protagonists are often stubborn or set in their ways. They do not want to change. Therefore, the storyteller-god must often be very cruel in its tactics. Stories are the most dramatic when the tests devised by the storyteller-god are at their most extreme. It helps to think of the storyteller-god as an incredibly impatient being. It has no time to wait for the protagonist to change slowly and gradually. So, it devises the harshest and sometimes most far-fetched scenario it can think of to force the desired change in the shortest period of time.

In *The Godfather,* Michael Corleone needs to accept the cold, pragmatic, and often dirty-handed means by which his world operates if he is to ever replace his father as the head of the Corleone family. To make Michael learn his lesson as quickly as possible, the storyteller-god creates a situation where Michael must take immediate action or else watch his loved ones die. This forces Michael to grow up very quickly in a very short period of time. With each successive incident, Michael yields more and more of his formerly flawed beliefs and transforms himself into the type of man he needs to be. In *The Bourne Identity,* Jason Bourne is a man who has lost his soul. He has willingly become an unthinking, unfeeling, killing machine for the CIA. To turn Bourne's life around, the storyteller-god takes the extreme step of giving Bourne amnesia. This situation forces Bourne to reexamine his life piece by piece and in the process discover the error of his ways. In *Back to the Future,* Marty McFly is a reckless teen who does not give any serious thought to his future. He needs to learn that his present actions will have future consequences. Impatient as always, the storyteller-god bends time and space itself to teach Marty this lesson in the most extreme way possible. Trapped thirty years in the past, Marty must learn how to think ahead and plan every action or else he will destroy the future and himself with it.

To conclude this point, the plot creates a situation perfectly matched to the protagonist's Internal Need. The very nature of its conflict demands the protagonist adopt the behaviors he or she desperately needs for a happier or more successful life. Using this approach, screenwriters can create narratives in which the Story Spine intertwines perfectly with the Character

Arc. The writer simply analyzes the story's protagonist, identifies his or her Fatal Flaw and Internal Need, and then designs an adventure where the nature of the conflict forces the protagonist to confront and then abandon that Flaw in order to gain the Need. In this way, plot serves character, not the other way around.

Yet this is not to say that the elements of every great cinematic story were necessarily realized in this order. It would be silly to assume that the creators of *Die Hard* originally wished to tell the story of a man who learns to face life's problems directly, and then created capering terrorists and rooftop explosions just to serve this purpose. It would be equally ridiculous to believe George Lucas cared only to tell a story of a boy who grows up to find his destiny and then invented the entire *Star Wars* universe for this effect. In these films, as in many, the idea for the plot premise undoubtedly came first. In such cases, a storyteller can still create a perfect fit between Story Spine and Character Arc by reversing the process described above. The writer simply considers the specific nature of the intended story conflict and identifies what personal quality a character must have to overcome it. Then, the writer creates a protagonist who lacks this quality at the start. Alternatively, the writer could identify a meaningful life benefit to be gained from the story's adventure and then create a protagonist who requires this benefit as his or her Internal Need. By this process, a cinematic storyteller can find the Character Arc best suited to fit any plot premise, or vice versa.

For the perfect balance between Story Spine and Character Arc, a direct causal relationship should exist between the Story Goal and Internal Need whereby one cannot be achieved without first attaining the other. In some stories, it is impossible for the protagonist to reach the Story Goal until he or she first acquires the Internal Need. In *The Godfather*, Michael Corleone cannot ensure his family's permanent safety until he first accepts the practical, cold-blooded mindset of a mafia don. In *The Matrix*, Neo cannot defeat the Agents until he believes in his unlimited potential. The reverse is equally effective. In many other stories, the Internal Need can only be obtained by first accomplishing the Story Goal. In *The Bourne Identity*, Jason Bourne cannot truly reclaim his soul until he faces and defeats his enemies at the

CIA. In *Rocky,* the title character cannot achieve his self-worth until he proves himself against Apollo Creed. In either case, the story's two primary structural objectives are contingent upon one another for success. Because their end destinations are inseparably linked, the Story Spine and Character Arc are intertwined in such a way that the structures must work together to reach their individual goals.

But what exactly is the structure by which the Story Spine and Character Arc interact? Furthermore, how does either structure make any progress with all the conflict standing in the protagonist's way? Left to their own devices, both the Story Spine and Character Arc can make little headway. In the plot, the protagonist encounters obstacles the he or she cannot overcome until the protagonist abandons his or her flawed attitudes, behaviors, or beliefs. Meanwhile in the Character Arc, the protagonist will not recognize the need to change until he or she receives enough evidence to prove that this change is an absolute necessity. Left this way, the story is stuck, both in terms of plot and character. To make any progress, the dimensions of plot and character must work together. The cinematic narrative creates a mutual solution to both structural problems by intertwining the Story Spine and Character Arc in such a way that each provides the keys to unlock the other's doors.

When the flawed protagonist encounters the Story Problem, he or she first chooses to react in his or her accustomed ways. Because these ways are inherently flawed in both thought and action, these early attempts do little to solve the story's problems. To the contrary, they make the situation worse. By pursuing objectives with ineffective methods or counter-productive behaviors, the protagonist essentially works against him or herself, causing difficulties to escalate and new problems to arise. If any real progress is made, it either comes with serious complications attached or is soon unraveled by later mistakes.

For the first half of the story, the protagonist is either ignorant of his or her errors or chooses to continue to act in a flawed manner in spite of them. However, these accumulated mistakes eventually come back to haunt the protagonist in a way he or she can no longer deny. The plot imposes a severe complication, usually at or near the story's Midpoint, that greatly worsens the situation and threatens to ruin or destroy the protagonist in the near future. The worst thing about this complication is that it is in some way the protagonist's own fault. My previous book named this event the "monster moment" in allusion to the story of Doctor Frankenstein.* Like Doctor Frankenstein, the protagonist's previous flawed actions have inadvertently triggered events that end up creating a figurative monster of the protagonist's own making. Now the monster comes to life, threatening to destroy the protagonist. This moment may take many forms. An act by the protagonist may provoke an overpowering response from the force of antagonism. (In *Braveheart*, William Wallace's refusal to negotiate in battle provokes King Edward Longshanks to use all his power to try to destroy Wallace. In *Raiders of the Lost Ark*, Indy's secret search for the Ark allows the antagonists to steal it right from under his nose.) Past mistakes may suddenly come home to roost. (*In Back to the Future*, Marty realizes that altering history now threatens to wipe him out of existence. In *The Shawshank Redemption*, Andy Dufresne discovers his entanglement in the Warden's crooked scheme blocks his one chance to prove his innocence.) Or the protagonist may simply find him or herself trapped in a dead-end situation from which further progress seems impossible. (In *Rocky*, Rocky Balboa's refusal of all help dooms him to humiliation against Apollo Creed. In *Star Wars*, the heroes' quest inadvertently traps them aboard the Death Star.) Whatever the case, the protagonist would not have found him or herself in this far more monstrous situation had it not been for the misguided or poorly thought-out actions he or she took before this point.

With this complication, the protagonist faces a Crucial Decision regarding how to proceed. The protagonist has three options. The first is to give up. However, this is unfeasible seeing as the Stakes have now grown far too high. The second option is to remain on the current path. Here the protagonist fails to acknowledge that past decisions have been in error. Instead, the protagonist redoubles his or her dedication to the Fatal Flaw and intensifies his or her negative behaviors under the belief that this extra effort will power through the new story problems. However, such methods

* See *Atoms*, Chapter 6

are what got the protagonist into this mess in the first place, and if chosen will only exacerbate problems further and ultimately lead to defeat. The protagonist's final option is to reevaluate past actions and seek a new path to overcome the current obstacles. Here the protagonist has the wisdom to realize that past actions have been foolish, ineffective, or counter-productive and in response chooses to experiment with new attitudes and behaviors radically different than those before. In other words, the plot's monster moment forces the protagonist to take his or her first tentative step toward personal change; not because the protagonist wants to, but because he or she must.

For those protagonists who do choose to adjust their behavior, a dramatic shift occurs in the relationship between character and plot. Until now, these two dimensions have seemed to work against one another. The protagonist's behavior has directly interfered with the plot's movement towards a positive resolution. Yet when the protagonist chooses to alter his or her behavior, he or she finds better, more productive means to move forward. Character and plot begin to cooperate. By adopting more suitable attitudes and behaviors, the protagonist begins to swim with the current of his or her world rather than against it, allowing him or her to overcome obstacles and unlock doors. Plot events have forced the beginnings of character change, and in turn this glimmer of change allows the plot to advance for the first time towards a positive rather than a negative resolution.

However, the protagonist certainly does not undergo any kind of instant, light-switch conversion. It would be unnatural to assume that any person would change the totality of his or her behavior based on the outcome of a single event. In truth, the amount of personal change at this point is minimal. The protagonist has only momentarily yielded from his or her old nature because the situation demands it. While the protagonist may have opened the door to the possibility of greater personal change, far more dramatic pressure is required to continue this transformation.

Once again, plot takes on this responsibility. The protagonist's new methods are challenged by an escalating series of threats and obstacles. Faced with these even greater challenges, the protagonist finds him or herself stuck in situations where the only way out is to forego more and more of his or her old attitudes and behaviors in favor of the new. With each success, the protagonist gains confidence in the new methods and becomes more willing to set aside those of the past. Fundamentally, the narrative develops by a simple pattern. Conflicts and obstacles demand greater character growth. Character growth overcomes the conflict or obstacle. The narrative advances because the Story Spine and Character Arc push each other forward in alternating fashion, obstacle by obstacle, step by step.

Yet despite all of this, the protagonist has not yet fully abandoned his or her Fatal Flaw. Though it may have been softened up a bit or had holes punched through it, the Flaw still lingers inside the character, tempting him or her to fall back on old ways. In moments of weakness, the protagonist may regress to past behaviors, leading to mistakes or failures the force of antagonism is more than willing to exploit. As long as the Flaw lingers, the protagonist will remain handicapped and unable to take the final steps necessary to reach the Story Goal. The protagonist becomes like a mountain climber attempting to reach a peak's summit while still weighed down by useless equipment. Unless cut free, this worthless burden will cause him or her to fall.

Often the protagonist must fall in order to learn his or her final lesson, and fall hard. Once again, the plot must intervene to complete character transformation. The process of action and counter-action between the protagonist and the force of antagonism eventually escalates to create what is known as a *crisis event.* This event (usually occurring at or near the end of Act 2B, but may arise much later), can take many forms: a costly failure, and impossible challenge, an enormous obstacle, an unexpected development that signals impending doom… Like the monster moment, the crisis event somehow stems from the protagonist's refusal to fully abandon the Fatal Flaw. While the protagonist may not be the direct cause of the crisis (the main culprit may be anything from the force of antagonism to pure bad luck), he or she still bears part of the blame. The protagonist could have avoided this crisis if only he or she had completely abandoned the remnants of the Fatal Flaw long ago. To force the protagonist to learn his or her final lesson, the crisis event is even more severe than the monster mo-ment before it. While the monster moment imposed a complication that with time may have eventually led to future doom, the crisis event threatens the protagonist with immediate and potentially irreversible defeat. If the protagonist cannot overcome this event, failure is certain.

Whereas the monster moment leads the protagonist to a Crucial Decision by which the process of change begins, the crisis event completes the protagonist's transformation by provoking a *moment of truth*. Facing the threat of irrevocable defeat, the protagonist is forced to fully recognize the consequences of hanging onto the Flaw and sees what actions are truly important or necessary to finally achieve the Story Goal. The paths to success or failure suddenly come into sharp focus. With this, the protagonist realizes victory is impossible as long as he or she clings onto the remnants of his or her past attitudes, behaviors, or beliefs and throws aside the fears and doubts that have caused him or her to do so. Once again, the protagonist does not do this because he or she wants to, but out of necessity. The pressure of story conflict demands the protagonist take this final step. Therefore, the moment of truth forces the protagonist to purge him or herself of the Flaw's remains and complete his or her transformation into a better, more capable individual.

With this last step in the Character Arc, the protagonist experiences a rebirth. No longer blinded by the Fatal Flaw, the protagonist enters the story's final battle fully empowered by the proper attitudes and behaviors necessary to overcome all remaining conflict and resolve the Story Problem. This transformation meets its ultimate test at the story climax. While the formerly flawed protagonist would have failed, the new and improved protagonist succeeds. Such a victory would have been impossible without personal change. The conclusion of the Character Arc allows for the conclusion of the Story Spine. These combined resolutions then provide the protagonist with his or her Internal Need. The two structures solve each other's problems.

* * *

Let's take a look at how this intertwining of structures operates in an actual film. I have chosen the 1988 action staple Die Hard as our example, chiefly because the dimension of character tends to be overlooked in such intensely paced genre films. Yet Die Hard stands out as superior in its genre, due largely in part to the influence of plot upon character and character upon plot.

Contrary to the stereotypical action hero, Die Hard's protagonist John McClane is hardly any kind of supercop. Though he is a trained police officer, he is an average joe who quite possibly has never been in serious danger in his life. In further contradiction of stereotype, John is a man who prefers to avoid direct conflict. This is established in the story's setup through John's relationship with his wife Holly. Serious marital issues have developed between John and Holly, but rather than address these problems directly, John avoids them with passive-aggression and quiet resentment. He does this partially out of stubbornness, but more so out of fear. Though John is a "toughguy," he fears taking risks which might make himself vulnerable. This is John's Fatal Flaw. By avoiding direct conflict, John worsens his marital problems, creating a barrier that blocks him from a healthy and emotionally-satisfying life with his family (John's Internal Need). John cannot reach his Need until he learns to face life's problems openly and directly.

To teach John his lesson, the story places him in a situation where he must either learn to face conflict directly or perish from the inability. As usual, this is the most extreme situation possible. Terrorists invade Nakatomi Tower and take Holly and the rest of its occupants hostage. While John is the only individual to avoid capture, he does not instantly adopt a heroic role. To the contrary, his first reaction is to run and hide. This is on account of his Fatal Flaw. John reacts to conflict by avoiding it. However, it soon becomes clear that this strategy will not do much good. John witnesses antagonist Hans Gruber execute Holly's boss Mr. Takagi and realizes he cannot simply wait for the situation to resolve itself. He must do something or else more people will die. With this, John commits to a Story Goal: to save Holly by defeating the terrorists.

Yet John's predicament is essentially an ironic contradiction. A man who instinctively avoids direct conflict must somehow overcome a situation that demands it. Because of his Fatal Flaw, John's first actions are weak and passive. His first idea is to pull the fire alarm in hope that emergency responders will arrive and resolve the problem. However, this weak action not only fails, but worsens John's situation. Hans is alerted to John's presence and sends a gunman to find him. John again reacts in a flawed, passive way. He attempts to arrest the gunman rather than attack him. This also backfires, triggering a fight that John survives only by accident.

These failures force John to put forth more effort. However, they are not yet enough to challenge his Flaw. John's next attempt to resolve the problem continues to sidestep direct confrontation. John tries to contact the police on a stolen radio. But once more, John's chosen methods worsen his situation. Hans overhears the mayday call and sends three men to kill John. Again, John runs rather than fights, initiating a chase sequence that eventually traps him like a rat.

So far, John's flawed choices have only made his situation worse and worse. He is spinning his wheels and getting nowhere. He needs to change his tactics. However, John is too set in his ways to come to this conclusion on his own. The only way John will learn this lesson is if he encounters a plot situation that demands it. So, the plot intervenes with the arrival of police officer Al Powell. While this is the opportunity John has been hoping for, there is a problem. Powell does not notice anything wrong. This forces John to take direct and decisive action to get Powell's attention, or else Powell will leave and John will lose his one chance to get help.

Yet John's Flaw trips him up again. He hesitates to immediately shoot the men who come to stop him from alerting Powell. Now, cornered by a gun-man with his one chance of hope slipping away, John is finally compelled to take the kind of bold action he has avoided thus far. He kills the gunman and catches Powell's attention in an extreme way. By finally taking direct action, John overcomes his current obstacle and advances the plot.

With this victory, you would think that John has learned his lesson. Direct, decisive action provides far better results than passivity and hesitation. Yet when the police arrive at the story's Midpoint, John mistakenly believes he can slide back into his accustomed behavior, find a good hiding place, and wait for a happy resolution. Past events may have challenged John's flawed methods, but they have done little to challenge the flawed mindset behind them. So far, all of John's actions have been orientated around getting police attention in hope that once the police arrive he will not have to take any further action. In other words, everything he has done has attempted to avoid resolving the problem directly. John still remains rooted in his Fatal Flaw. To force John to change, a major plot event must prove to John that his attitude is wrong and his former actions misguided. Enter the story's monster moment.

Contrary to John's expectations, the police turn out to be arrogant incompetents who will only get more innocent people killed. John's eager efforts to hand off responsibility to someone else have made the situation far worse than it was before. With this unexpected development, John faces a dilemma. If he remains passive, the police will bungle the operation. Yet if he takes any more direct action, he will put himself at extreme risk. The Stakes are too high for John to rely on the first option. So John has no choice but to do what he never dreamed of before: face the force of antagonism directly and resolve the problem on his own.

However, choosing a new path is one thing. Following that path is another. Internal change requires external motivation. Without such motivation, John would have no legitimate reason to continue his transformation. So, the plot imposes a series of conflicts, threats, and obstacles (from the villains inside the building as well as the authorities outside) that force John to come out of hiding and face problems directly. He does not do this because he wants to. He does this because he is forced by the plot's intensifying situation. Yet with each incident, John progresses in his personal growth. The old passive John slowly disappears and is replaced by a strong-willed solitary hero.

Yet though John has grown, his old habits die hard (sorry, I couldn't resist). When a twist of fate places John one-on-one with Hans Gruber, a bold, decisive move could put a quick end to the Story Problem. Yet John once again hesitates, allowing time for his enemies to get the drop on him. The ensuing shoot-out leaves John limping away, bloodied and momentarily defeated. John meets this setback due to his failure to fully commit to the required personal change. Part of him still does not want to face the conflict directly and hopes that if he can just hang tough the situation will resolve itself. John must be purged of this belief. Otherwise, he will continue to fail.

For John to complete his transformation, he must experience a moment of truth, and such moments can only come through a crisis event. This event arrives when John discovers the final phase of Hans' master plan at the end of Act 2B. Hans plans to escape the authorities by killing all the hostages. With only minutes before this occurs, John faces a legitimate crisis. He can no longer wait. He can no longer hesitate. He can no longer hope for outside assistance. He must take it upon himself to save everyone's life, and he must do it *now*.

John responds to this crisis by throwing all remaining doubts or fears out the window and hurling himself into battle with frenzied abandon. Not because he wants to, but because he must. One by one, John faces and defeats his remaining challenges head-on. Purged of his former weakness, John meets Hans at the story's final climax and proves his transformation by shooting Hans without fear or hesitation. With this, John saves Holly and achieves his Story Goal.

Plot events have turned John into a man who no longer fears facing life's problems directly. This personal change opens the door to John's Internal Need. When John reunites with Holly, we are given a sense that their marital problems are also on a road to resolution now that John has learned to abandon his old ways. The events of plot have caused the transformation of character. The transformation of character has resolved the events of the plot. The combination allows the hero to live happily ever after.

As it turns out, all of this can be expressed far more simply. Viewed from a larger sociological perspective, the interaction between Story Spine and Character Arc follows a very basic archetype, one mirrored in Hollywood storytelling's most recent ancestor—the fairy tale. By analyzing these older tales and comparing them to modern cinematic storytelling, we find that the protagonist's journey to success or failure typically comes down to a simple thing: a battle between *pride* and *humility.*

## THE HUMILITY ARC

Whether realized or not, American storytelling has been profoundly influenced by the fairy tales of Western Europe. Thanks to the wide-scale immigration of the 19th and 20th centuries, along with the successful publication of these stories by Josef and Wilhelm Grimm (originally published in 1812), these Old World morality tales have been the first narratives taught to American children for generations. Even today, young imaginations continue to be sparked by the likes of "Cinderella," "Jack & the Beanstalk," or "Little Red Riding Hood."

The Hollywood film appears to be the fairy tale's direct descendant. Despite the desire to see cinema as something far more modern or refined, the form and content of the Hollywood feature film still has far more in common with an expanded fairy tale than it does with the novel or the traditional theatre. Though Hollywood filmmaking has matured into an art form capable of serious, sophisticated, and often complex communication, one connecting thread remains unbroken from its predecessor: the fairy tale's concept of heroic identity.

The word "hero" is typically laden with valiant connotations. It is usually appended to the brave and strong, figures who seem almost god-like compared to our lowly selves. Yet according to Harvard Folklore and Mythology Professor Dr. Maria Tatar, the hero of the fairy tale (particularly those of the Grimm tales) is routinely defined by a far more unexpected quality—Humility.

Humility turns out to be the divine virtue of the fairy tale world. Fate shines favorably on those who are humble and punishes those who are not. In her book *The Hard Facts of the Grimms' Fairy Tales,* Tatar identifies two patterns repeated with general consistency throughout the Grimm collection. In Type A, the hero is anything but strong and valiant. To the contrary, these characters are usually simple-minded fools, poor peasants, or helpless children. Rather than strength of arms or keenness of wit, these heroes are set apart by an absolute lack of guile or pretension. When the hero demonstrates this quality through humble acts of kindness, obedience, or self-denial, he or she catches the attention of an outside, often magical force. This force rewards the hero with the tools, assistance, or abilities necessary to overcome the story's problems. Sometimes, this intercession is simply a rescue at the story's end, as in "Little Red Riding Hood." More often, the assistance comes early, as in "Cinderella" or "Jack & the Beanstalk," leading to an adventure through which the hero receives an ultimate reward.

In contrast, tales in Type B contain heroes who begin arrogant, haughty, or selfish. These characters suffer from the sin of pride. Pride is humility's opposite. If humility is divine, then pride must be wicked. The simplest of these stories merely show how such behavior is punished, as in "Goldilocks & the Three Bears." The more sophisticated, such as "The Princess & the Frog" or "Rumpelstiltskin," dramatize a scenario through which the hero's pride is *broken*. The hero is subjected to a series of humiliating tasks or episodes that strip the character of his or her prideful nature. As soon as the character accepts a state of humility, he or she is rewarded by outside intervention and granted a happy end.

Though these tales may seem utterly simplistic, closer inspection reveals that the basic pattern of humility followed by reward has been adopted with near universality into the structure of the Hollywood film. The only difference is that Hollywood overwhelmingly prefers Type B over Type A. Though Hollywood protagonists face daunting physical obstacles in their quests, time and again the real barrier to happiness and success comes from the hero's own selfish pride. Victory comes to the protagonist only once pride is abandoned.

Though modern usage has given the word certain positive connotations, "pride" has traditionally meant the act of elevating one's conception of self above others. It is the sin of self-importance. Hence for our purposes, pride should be broadly defined to mean any fractured, inflated, or self-serving view of oneself that runs contrary to the necessities of the story world. A more psychologically-accurate term would be "ego-centrism," the act of seeing one's own cares and needs as more important than all others.

Pride creates a barrier isolating the protagonist from reality. A bubble of ignorance or self-delusion surrounds the character, precluding him or her from any genuine understanding, connection, or constructive influence upon the world. Unless the bubble is broken, the character will remain unable to see things as they really are, leaving him or her incapable of overcoming the story's problems. In *Rocky,* the title character's trampled-upon pride causes him to reject any offer of help for his fight against Apollo Creed. In *Shrek,* a blow to the hero's personal pride causes him to turn his back on the woman he loves. In *The Sixth Sense,* Dr. Malcolm Crowe's professional pride prevents him from believing that Cole can see dead people.

To overcome this, reality must penetrate the bubble. Story events chip away at pride's tough shell until it ultimately breaks. Harsh reality floods inside, and the hero is humiliated to acknowledge how foolish, misguided, or harmful his or her former perceptions have been. In *Casablanca,* Rick's wounded pride compels him to refuse help to Ilsa and Lazlo at their time of need. But with time and pressure, Rick realizes he is acting the heel, harming not only the woman he loves, but the entire Allied cause in the process. In *Schindler's List,* Oskar Schindler's elevated self-importance allows him to believe there is no harm in exploiting the Jews of Poland. But after witnessing repeated atrocities, Oskar must admit he is on the wrong side of good and evil. In *The Matrix,* Neo resists the role of humanity's savior, preferring to remain a reluctant outsider. Eventually, events cause Neo to realize he indeed has a heroic destiny he must not deny.

With pride's bubble shattered, the hero realizes there are higher ideals at play; ideals far more important than his or her selfish concerns. The hero is humbled by this and in response abandons all personal interest. The hero is then reborn a servant of the higher ideal, a person willing and able to sacrifice all things for a greater cause. Rick gives up the life he has created in Casablanca to help Isla and Lazlo escape. Oskar Schindler sacrifices every ill-gotten penny to save his workers' lives. Neo surrenders his previous identity to become humanity's savior. Pride blinds heroes. Humility opens their eyes to a far more righteous path.

Every hero undergoes this transformation. Even when a character appears meek of will or pure of heart, some ego-centric delusion, large or small, prevents him or her from offering the selfless surrender necessary for heroism. Frodo in *Lord of the Rings: The Fellowship of the Ring* is a hobbit. As a hobbit, he has been taught to believe his folk are above meddling in the outside world. When burdened with the protection of the One Ring, Frodo wants nothing more than to hand the ring over to someone else so he may return home, essentially rejecting his role as hero. Andy Dufresne in *The Shawshank Redemption* may be shy and soft-spoken, but he behaves as if his innocence places him above the world around him, an attitude which eventually causes his downfall. Jason Bourne in *The Bourne Identity* sees himself as an innocent victim, something he is not. This misconception puts actual innocents in harm's way. As with all other heroes, these prideful illusions must be stripped away before the character can surrender him or herself to the higher ideal and take the proper actions to set the world right again.

Yet as the proverb states, "Pride goeth before destruction." Some protagonists foolishly hang onto some or all of their pride until the last moment and thus risk ultimate defeat. In *Star Wars,* it is not until Luke is dead in the sights of Darth Vader's TIE fighter that he finally stops trying to succeed by his own means and surrenders his will to the Force. In *Raiders of the Lost Ark,* it is not until the Ark of the Covenant is opened that Indiana Jones realizes he has been meddling with a power far greater than himself and closes his eyes to what he is not worthy to see. Lester Burnham in *American Beauty* narrowly avoids cinematic damnation with a last-second realization of how foolish and reckless his pursuit of teenage Angela has been. These late-occurring crisis events lead to deathbed conversions, turning certain failure into a surprise victory.

Yet still, there are protagonists who refuse to abandon their pride and meet their doom because of it. It is by a failure to relinquish self-destructive pride that *Scarface*'s Tony Montana meets his bloody death, *Citizen Kane*'s Charles Foster Kane his bitter isolation, and *Amadeus*'s Salieri his incurable madness. Like every other protagonist, these characters also end their stories deeply humbled, but in these cases humility comes only after irrevocable defeat. Every Hollywood protagonist reaches humility at one point or another. The only difference between victory and failure is how and when this transition occurs.

To conclude, Hollywood filmmaking's use of the Humility Arc continues a centuries-old narrative tradition. Like the fairy tale, Hollywood stories continually prove humility to be society's divine virtue and pride its ultimate sin. This, when simplified to its core, is the functional purpose of the interaction between the Story Spine and Character Arc. Every Hollywood story repeats a lesson we have been taught since nursery school. Success comes to the unselfish. To be heroic, one must first be humble.

## THE INCLUSION OF THEME

To reiterate the previous chapter, the theme, being abstract and invisible, depends upon plot and character to deliver its meaning. Filmmakers may use more explicit devices to suggest meaning overtly, but these can only be embellishments upon the ideological conflicts already present within the Story Spine and Character Arc. A proper thematic message is delivered through the story's dramatic action, not through external application.

Like the interaction between the Story Spine and Character Arc, the Thematic Argument shares a symbiotic relationship with the structures of plot and character. However, the nature of this relationship is somewhat different. While the Story Spine and Character Arc possess a progressive relationship where the development of one allows for the advancement of the other, interactions with the Thematic Argument are based more upon the services one structure provides for the other.

The Thematic Argument, with its demand that every narrative element serve the secondary purpose of representing either the theme or anti-theme, provides all elements of plot and character with an ideological unity. It presents criteria to decide what events, actions, and behaviors are relevant to the story's particular message, and at the same time prevents the narrative from skewing off course by eliminating any content that may be irrelevant or inconsequential. The Spine and Arc return this favor by communicating the theme's abstract message through physical actions the audience can observe and understand. In this way, the structures serve one another with no detectable separation in between.

The Thematic Argument also offers a secondary benefit to both plot and character by allowing opportunities to enrich the basic narrative with dramatic subplots. Subplots add complexity to the plot as well as possibilities for deeper exploration of character. However, this is not a subplot's primary purpose. Subplots exist to examine the argument between theme and anti-theme from multiple situations or contexts. The main story conflict addresses the Thematic Argument from only one angle. By adding subplots, the theme and anti-theme may be evaluated from other perspectives. This provides more depth and breadth to the Thematic Argument, resulting in a story with a fuller and more conclusive message. While subplots may at times be only tangentially-related to the protagonist's pursuit of the Story Goal, these sidelines of action are still bound to the main narrative by the fact that they explore the same thematic battle. In this way, the Thematic Argument allows for a greater diversity of story content while still keeping the narrative an ideologically-unified whole.

But which comes first in the storytelling process? Should a storyteller begin with a theme and then create physical events to express it? Or should plot and character come first, with the expectation that meaning will arise through them? In other words, does the theme come from the story, or does the story come from the theme? Like the enigma of the chicken and the egg, both approaches are equally viable. A storyteller may begin his or her work concerned only with the elements of plot and character, and then later identify what thematic values may be at play within the story's conflicts. This approach allows the theme to emerge organically. If the storyteller takes this route, he or she must eventually seek out the emergent thematic battle and then shape content around it so a proper Thematic Argument will form. Otherwise, the story's action may lack ideological focus and its message will remain unclear. Conversely, a storyteller may begin with a thematic message already in mind and then invent dramatic conflicts to express it. Whether a storyteller begins with the chicken or the egg does not really matter as long as one element emerges from the other. Either approach will provide a structural unity between the story's visible and invisible components.*

## THE THEMATIC MATRIX

As mentioned at the conclusion of Chapter 1-3, the Thematic Argument expresses its ultimate meaning through the use of a two-part structure. This two-part structure is essentially a combination of the two most important events of the Character Arc and Story Spine. First comes the Character Arc's moment of Crucial Decision. When the protagonist chooses to abandon the Fatal Flaw for the sake of personal change or reject personal change in favor of the Flaw, the protagonist essentially chooses to embrace either the theme or the anti-theme. Second comes the plot's final climax. Through victory or failure, this event proves whether the protagonist's choice was correct. As we can see, these two events are causally connected. If the protagonist chooses to side with the correct thematic value at the Crucial Decision, he or she will be rewarded with victory at the final climax. If the protagonist sides with the incorrect value, he or she is punished with failure at the story's end. By presenting a choice, and then illustrating the positive or negative outcome of that choice, the story delivers a message regarding the selected value.

From a structural perspective, the debate between theme and anti-theme is fairly simple. One is a correct value that will lead to victory. The other is an incorrect value that will lead to failure. However, the audience views this debate in a much different way. To viewers, the Thematic Argument is a

---

* While both approaches are indeed viable, I urge beginning screenwriters to prefer the organic option. When taken with an inexperienced hand, the theme-first approach often forefronts the message too plainly, resulting in clumsy or heavy-handed communication that will interfere with an enjoyable narrative. Great skill and subtlety is required with the theme-first approach, and is therefore best left to the more experienced.

battle between a value they *endorse* (based upon their personal, cultural, or social beliefs) and a value they must *reject* (based upon those same beliefs). To structure, the Thematic Argument is about what behaviors are necessary to achieve victory. To the audience, the Thematic Argument is about what behaviors are right or wrong. Yet as we are about to see, these two perspectives do not always match. Sometimes the paths that lead to victory or failure run contrary to the audience's moral or ethical expectations.

To fully understand the Thematic Argument's ultimate expression of meaning, let us first break things down to their simplest elements. The Crucial Decision has two possible outcomes: the protagonist chooses to align with a socially-approved value (one the audience endorses) or the protagonist chooses to align with a socially-disapproved value (one the audience rejects). The final climax also has two possible outcomes: the protagonist wins or the protagonist loses. When these variables are combined, it creates four potential story resolutions:

1. The protagonist chooses an approved value and succeeds.
2. The protagonist chooses an approved value and fails.
3. The protagonist chooses a disapproved value and succeeds.
4. The protagonist chooses a disapproved value and fails.

These outcomes can be visually illustrated in what I call the Four-Way Thematic Matrix:

|  | Socially approved value | Socially disapproved value |
|---|---|---|
| Victory | Celebratory | Cynical |
| Failure | Tragic | Cautionary |

When broken down as such, the Thematic Matrix raises important questions. If the underlying sociological purpose of storytelling is to encourage
proper social behaviors by dramatizing a character's success or failure, why
would a story punish a hero for embracing a value the audience considers
good and meaningful? Furthermore, why would a story allow a character
to succeed through behaviors the audience has been taught to consider
harmful or wrong? Does this not give viewers the wrong message? Is this
not socially irresponsible on the part of the storyteller? Does this not
contradict storytelling's intended purpose? The answer, essentially, is no.

As suggested by the earlier paragraph, there are two dimensions to the
Thematic Argument's dramatic resolution: a structural dimension and an
audience dimension. The structural dimension pertains simply to whether
the protagonist meets success or failure. The audience dimension pertains
to whether the audience perceives this success or failure to be fair or deserved.

It is through this combination that the story expresses its message upon the thematic value in question. Audiences, as members of a culture or society, possess certain beliefs as to what is good or bad, right or wrong, fair or unfair. The story's structural resolution may reinforce or contradict the audience's beliefs. When the audience sees a character succeed by embracing a value they endorse or fail by embracing a value they must reject, these outcomes reinforce the audience's beliefs. They see the outcome as fair and deserved. However, if a story shows how a socially-supported value can lead a character to failure, or even worse how a socially-condemned value can lead to victory, the story performs the more sophisticated task of questioning or challenging the audience's beliefs. The audience sees these outcomes as unfair or undeserved, provoking reflection upon the worth or veracity of the thematic value and in turn the beliefs they attach to it.

Why might a storyteller do this? The answer is simple. Through outlets such as school, family, government, and the media, each of us have been taught to think and feel certain ways about certain things. Every culture or society promotes a specific set of behavioral or ideological ideals. Yet the world does not always practice what it preaches. Individuals, cultures, and societies alike can become misguided, confused, or corrupted. No society is perfect, and therefore contradictions and hypocrisies often abound in which values upheld in principle fail to be rewarded in action. What is worse, cultures or societies may enforce beliefs that are in fact untrue, inaccurate, or counter-productive. These beliefs cause harm and may lead the world in the wrong direction. In free societies where individuals are allowed the right to question and criticize social institutions, artists take on the role of ideological guardians. Philosophically speaking, art is traditionally considered a search for truth. The artist examines an aspect of the world or the human condition and expresses his or her personal conclusion through his or her work. If the artist's perception of truth contradicts the "truth" promoted by a culture or society, the artist sees it as his or her duty to point out this contradiction. By revealing such falsehoods, failures, or hypocrisies, the artist hopes to bring the issue to the receiver's attention, challenge flawed beliefs, and promote positive social or cultural change.

In this regard, a cinematic storyteller may use his or her art form to perform one of two social functions. If the storyteller agrees with a prevailing social or cultural belief, he or she may promote that belief by showing how the socially-approved value always leads to victory or how its opposing socially-disapproved value always leads to failure. These stories urge individuals to strengthen their dedication to socially or culturally supported values so our world may maintain its present state or improve itself by remaining on its assigned course. If the storyteller disagrees with a prevailing social or cultural belief or finds fault in its implementation, he or she may question or criticize that belief by showing how a value the culture or society approves may lead to harm or how the world often gives greater reward to those who embrace values the culture or society traditionally condemns. These stories suggest that the world is botched or broken and encourage viewers to reevaluate their perceptions or beliefs.

To illustrate with examples, both *Rocky* and *Raging Bull* uphold existing social beliefs. In the former, the protagonist is rewarded for adopting attitudes and behaviors our society considers virtuous. In the latter, the protagonist is punished for clinging to attitudes and behaviors our society considers harmful. From both, the audience receives clear lessons on how one should or should not behave. While the viewer may have already known that one behavior is considered good and the other bad, these stories reinforce those existing beliefs by providing concrete examples of the potential reward or punishment that may come from them. Like behavioral modification therapy, the audience is led to mentally associate good outcomes with one set of behaviors and bad outcomes with the other, potentially motivating them to subconsciously gravitate towards the former and avoid the latter.

In contrast, *Chinatown* and *The Godfather* criticize prevailing social beliefs with outcomes contradictory to moral or ethical expectations. In *Chinatown*, a virtuous protagonist is defeated by a corrupted world. While the protagonist adheres to a socially-approved value, his actions still lead to failure. This suggests that society is flawed. It does not in fact reward a value it supposedly supports. In *The Godfather*, the protagonist finds victory through attitudes and behaviors society traditionally insists can only lead to ruin.

This story suggests that the framework of virtues promoted by society is an illusion or lie. The world actually operates by a different system of reward and punishment, one that does more harm than good. Yet despite these outcomes, these films have no intention of encouraging audiences to follow the characters' behavioral examples as seen in *Rocky* or *Raging Bull*. Their messages are far more social than personal. By providing outcomes that negate prevailing social beliefs, these stories point out a schism that has developed between belief and actuality. They hope for viewers to recognize and then attempt to correct the ways our world has gone wrong rather than allow our culture or society to continue its misguided ways.

As previously explained, the two factors contributing to the Thematic Matrix (the protagonist's choice between a socially-approved value or a socially-disapproved value, and the protagonist's success or failure at the story's end) combined to create four possible narrative conclusions. These conclusions create stories of four general THEMATIC TYPES, each expressing a different kind of message and eliciting a different emotional response from its audience. Listed in order from the most socially-affirming to the most socially-critical, we will name these types the CELEBRATORY, the CAUTIONARY, the TRAGIC, and the CYNICAL.

1. *The Celebratory*      (examples: *Back to the Future, Rocky, The Shawshank Redemption*)  The protagonist adopts a socially-approved value and succeeds because of it. The majority of Hollywood films belong to this type. By dramatizing a scenario in which a socially-approved value leads to victory, these stories glorify the value as something we should consider important or meaningful. The Celebratory provides a simple moral lesson. Do what is considered correct, and good things will happen. As a result, viewers are encouraged to adopt the story's value into their own lives.

2. *The Cautionary*    (examples: *Raging Bull, Amadeus, Citizen Kane*) The protagonist embraces a socially-disapproved value and fails because of it. Whereas the Celebratory glorifies, the Cautionary demonizes. By showing how characters meet defeat or misfortune by

rejecting socially-approved behaviors, the Cautionary urges viewers not to follow the same path. These stories act as warnings to the audience. Fail to behave in a correct manner, and one will fail in life as well.

3. *The Tragic*  (examples: *Chinatown, Braveheart, One Flew Over the Cuckoo's Nest*)  The protagonist embraces a socially-approved value yet fails on account of it. The message found in the Tragic is a bit more complicated. While it still upholds the socially-approved value as something good or meaningful, the fact that the story fails to reward the hero suggests that society is currently out of line with a value it supposedly holds dear. The result is social criticism. Faced with what is perceived as an unfair end, the audience is forced to recognize the injustices or hypocrisies within our society.

4. *The Cynical*  (examples: *The Godfather, The Silence of the Lambs, Apocalypse Now*)\*  The protagonist adopts a socially-disapproved value and succeeds because of it. These stories present the darkest and most unsettling of tales. By showing how characters find greater success by embracing what society considers immoral or wrong, Cynical narratives suggest that our moral or ethical systems may be illusions or lies. These stories do more than point out hypocrisy. They imply that our world is fundamentally broken. Viewers are compelled to contemplate whether there is truth in what the story suggests and if a solution can be found.

In conclusion, the Thematic Argument delivers its final message through the combined outcomes of the Character Arc and Story Spine. The protagonist chooses a value to live by, and then meets victory or failure on account of that choice, resulting in one of four thematic resolutions. As with most concepts in screencraft, these four categories are flexible enough to allow for great variety in both form and content. In what manner or intensity a social value is upheld or denounced all remain dependent upon the particular story and the intent of the individual storyteller. Likewise, the

\* These twelve examples will be examined in detail in Chapter 1-6.

theme's final verdict may be utterly decisive or, like many lessons encountered in real life, remain clouded in doubt or ambiguity.* Because of this flexibility, every traditionally-told Hollywood or American Independent film conceivably fits into one of these four thematic types, regardless of tone, style, genre, or premise. Despite superficial differences, every well-written film expresses its ultimate meaning in the same consistent way; through the combined outcomes of Story Spine, Character Arc, and Thematic Argument.

Until now, we have approached the cinematic narrative's three primary structures one at a time, as if they were separate and individual components functioning in cooperation. Yet as previously explained, cinematic stories are holistic in nature. A well-told story unfolds as a singular line of action in which the dimensions of plot, character, and theme meld together as one. This implies that there must be a structure unifying these dimensions. A structure that guides all other structures. A superstructure, if you will.

Finding this superstructure requires a fresh perspective. We must no longer think of the cinematic narrative as a combination of elements, but as a unified whole. We must not focus upon the separate concepts, but the principles which unite them. Furthermore, we must take into consideration every possible cinematic narrative of traditional form, regardless of genre, content, style, or tone. With this approach, we may discover the basic, all-inclusive, and potentially universal form by which virtually every successful Hollywood or American Independent narrative operates. Now that the basic theoretical groundwork has been laid, we can finally move on to our final step and build a unified theory of narrative structure.

* See Chapter 1-7 for cases in which thematic ambiguity may be desirable.

*Works cited in this chapter:*
Tatar, Maria. The Hard Facts of the Grimms' Fairy Tales. *Princeton: Princeton University Press, 2003.*

# CHAPTER 1-5
## THREE BECOMES ONE:
# THE UNIFIED NARRATIVE STRUCTURE

We will begin right where we left off. The previous chapter concluded with the introduction of the Four-Way Thematic Matrix. To review, its basic assertion is that a story's thematic message is ultimately expressed by the combined outcomes of the Character Arc and Story Spine. The protagonist's Character Arc has two possible outcomes—the protagonist either embraces a value approved by society or one disapproved. The Story Spine also has two possible outcomes—the protagonist either achieves victory at the story's end or meets failure. When combined, these two variables result in one of four thematic resolutions (Celebratory, Cautionary, Tragic, or Cynical). This resolves the Thematic Argument with a conclusive message regarding the story's opposing values.

As it turns out, this model does more than illustrate the expression of theme. For starters, the Thematic Matrix presents the method by which the seemingly separate structures of plot, character, and theme ultimately converge to communicate a single meaning. As such, if there is indeed a structure unifying the Story Spine, Character Arc, and Thematic Argument into a cohesive whole, our investigation should start here.

If we begin at this ultimate point of convergence and work backwards, it quickly becomes apparent that the Thematic Matrix does more than delineate four possible narrative resolutions. It in fact defines four basic categories of narrative in general. The narratives of the Celebratory, Cautionary, Tragic, and Cynical types are all defined by the decisive outcomes of their Character Arc and Story Spine. However, these outcomes do not occur by spontaneous accord. They are the logical results of the entire chain of events that has occurred before them. In a well-written story, there is not a single element of plot that does not exist to move the narrative towards the final climax. Nor is there a single element of character that does not exist to compel the protagonist to accept or reject personal change. With all events focused upon the decisive conclusions of the Character Arc and Story Spine, it can be rationally claimed that the course and content of the narrative is at all times dictated by its intended thematic resolution. All narrative events propel the story towards a Celebratory, Cautionary, Tragic, or Cynical end. As such, the Celebratory, Cautionary, Tragic, and Cynical should not only be thought of as four thematic types, but the four basic varieties of narrative.

Yet if all traditionally-told cinematic stories can indeed be defined by one of these four categories of narrative, would this not mean that cinematic storytelling must have four overarching narrative structures, one for each thematic type, and not just a single structure as the title of this chapter suggests? After all, there seems to be clear disparities between the stories of the Celebratory, Cautionary, Tragic, and Cynical types in terms of their form, tone, and content. However, this is not the case. In all four narrative types, the dramatic structure is *exactly the same,* with the exception of one pivotal factor.

Let's take another look at the cinematic narrative's four possible resolutions:

*Celebratory*: The protagonist embraces a socially-approved value and succeeds.
*Cautionary*: The protagonist embraces a socially-disapproved value and fails.
*Tragic*: The protagonist embraces a socially-approved value and fails.
*Cynical*: The protagonist embraces a socially-disapproved value and succeeds.

At first glance, the stories of each group seem extremely dissimilar. It is as if all narratives are split into four polar directions, as far from one another as north is from south or east is from west. Yet commonalities do exist. To find the thread that connects all four, we must begin with a simple question: which of these categories are the most alike?

Our first impulse may be to group these categories according to their shared moral or ethical dimensions. In this sense, the Celebratory might be grouped with the Cautionary since both suggest a just world where good is rewarded and evil punished; or the Celebratory with the Tragic as both feature a virtuous hero fighting for what society considers good or meaningful. However, few structural parallels can be found with these combinations. This is because any attempt to analyze structure from a moral or ethical perspective essentially barks up the wrong tree. Like mathematics or the laws of nature, structure is a morally and ethically neutral thing. It does not think or feel. It is merely a functional process bound by simple rules. Judgments regarding good or bad and right or wrong are irrelevant. These judgments come from the audience dimension of storytelling, not the structural. As with math or the natural sciences, an investigation of narrative structure must focus solely upon physical results. In other words, the only thing of importance to structure is the literal outcome of narrative events. With a sole focus on outcome, only one question is truly relevant: does the hero *win* or does the hero *lose?* Using this criteria, the Celebratory should be grouped with the Cynical (both ending in victory), and the Cautionary with the Tragic (both ending in defeat).

As strange as it seems with their contradictory tones and thematic intentions, the Celebratory and Cynical demonstrate an identical narrative structure. In both, the protagonist is thrust into a dramatic conflict, bringing with him or her a flawed perspective which renders the character incapable of fully overcoming the story's problems. Eventually, dramatic pressure forces the protagonist to abandon his or her former perspective to adopt a more productive mindset. Through this, the protagonist transforms into a more capable individual with the attitudes and abilities necessary to defeat the story's conflict and claim victory at the end. In both the

Celebratory and the Cynical, the protagonist wins because he or she accepts the necessity of personal change.

Yet as similar as their structures may be, clear differences exist between the stories of the Celebratory and Cynical types. In the Celebratory, the hero succeeds by adopting socially-approved qualities, transforming the character into what the audience considers a "better" person. In the Cynical, the protagonist succeeds by taking on qualities society traditionally rejects, transforming the character into what the audience may consider a "worse" person. However, these two scenarios are not all that different. In both cases, the protagonist does not commit to this change because he or she wishes. The protagonist does so out of necessity. The character is merely doing what must be done to survive. In the cinematic story, survival requires change. But whether the protagonist must change for the "better" or the "worse" is not up to the character. This is decided by the character's world.

Celebratory narratives present "Worlds of Light." These are morally-idealized universes designed to reward values we traditionally consider good or just. To succeed, the protagonist must adopt these values, becoming what society would consider a better person. As a result, the audience feels good about the story's conclusion. It reinforces what they believe to be right. In contrast, Cynical narratives operate within "Worlds of Darkness." To survive in these environments, characters must adopt values we traditionally consider harmful or wrong. Conventional morality has no place in these worlds. It must be put aside if characters hope to succeed. These stories usually leave audiences with a bad taste in their mouths as the outcome contradicts what they would prefer to believe. Hence we see that the Celebratory and the Cynical exist as mirror opposites. They are identical in structure, yet morally or ethically reversed.

A samesuch relationship exists between the Cautionary and the Tragic. In both, the protagonist ultimately fails due to a refusal to conform his or her behavior to a required set of attitudes or beliefs. Rather than abandon the Fatal Flaw and adopt a new value, the protagonist clings to the Flaw out of a belief that he or she can defeat the story world through it. By refusing to alter his or her path, the protagonist is defeated.

The differences between the Cautionary and the Tragic again come from a reversal in moral polarity. Like in the Celebratory, Cautionary narratives present worlds that operate according to rules our society considers morally or ethically just. The protagonist meets his or her doom by ignoring these rules and clinging to a "destructive flaw" (an attitude or behavior our society considers incorrect). The audience approves of the protagonist's ultimate punishment because the character has refused to conform his or her behavior to what they consider to be "right." In contrast, the Tragic (like the Cynical) exists in a world which is morally-backwards. Here, the protagonist fails due to a "virtuous flaw." He or she clings to a value or quality the audience considers good or heroic. However, this trait stands in opposition to the warped value system of the story world. This world ignores the virtue and rewards its opposite. Because of this, the protagonist is destined to fail, no matter how good or honorable his or her intentions may be. The audience disapproves of this ending. In their eyes, the protagonist did everything right, yet is punished because of it. Note that though the structures are exactly the same, the audience's emotional reaction greatly differs due to the outside application of their own attitudes and beliefs. They approve of the protagonist's punishment in the Cautionary, yet disapprove of the same end in the Tragic. Yet in both, the protagonist fails for the same reason. He or she refused to conform his or her behavior to the expectations of the story world.

Here we begin to see that the audience's interpretation of a story's meaning results from a collision between the ethics of the story world and the viewer's personal, cultural, or social beliefs. If the story world rewards what the viewer believes should be rewarded or punishes what the viewer believes should be punished, the story reinforces the viewer's beliefs and urges him or her to continue to behave in the way culture or society has taught him or her to believe is right. But if the outcome contradicts moral or ethical expectations, viewers are led to question their beliefs as well as the culture or society that promotes them.

For such a collision to occur, the moral or ethical systems of story worlds must *exist independently* from the audience's own. Stories do not express meaning by presenting the audience with a world identical to the one in which they live. Rather, stories encourage viewers to reflect upon their own world by presenting an *alternative* world to compare it to. Why? The reason is simple. On the most basic cognitive level, meaning is found through an observation of differences. The viewer observes the state of one thing, compares it to the state of another thing, and draws a conclusion from the difference. Stories exist within separate worlds with their own separate value systems. These systems may be similar to that of the viewer or may differ drastically. The audience perceives meaning by comparing and contrasting the two worlds. How are the worlds the same? How are they different? What does the fictional world have that our world lacks? What does the fictional world lack that our world has? Based on these observations, the audience forms conclusions regarding their world, their personal behaviors, and how both may be changed for the better or worse.

Two practical aspects of screencraft require special attention here. The first is how a storyteller creates this moral or ethical contrast. The second is what is actually meant by a flaw or "negative" character trait. Both of these issues regard the principle of *moral relativism*.

When an audience encounters a story, they bring with them a host of presumptions as to what should be considered good or bad, positive or negative, socially-uplifting or socially-destructive. Most of these beliefs have a cultural basis. Every culture constructs a value system based upon widely-shared attitudes and beliefs, and from this establishes codes of behavior to define what actions are proper and which are not. This allows members of a culture to coexist in relative harmony as they are all generally of the same mind. However, value systems and codes of behavior differ from one culture to the next. This often creates conflict when cultural groups interact. Yet this does not mean that one group is right and the other is wrong. Both perspectives are equally valid. Conflict arises from the fact that value systems and codes of behavior are morally relativistic. All notions of morals or ethics are relative to the principles or beliefs upheld by their originating culture. This means all values are open to subjectivity. There is no universal "right" or "wrong." These are only words we use to assign judgment based on our prevailing cultural beliefs.

Storytellers can take advantage of moral relativism for the purpose of artistic communication. Though a story may imitate reality closely enough to mislead us into believing it exists in the same world as our own, this is never the actual case. Stories exist in separate worlds, and as such function by their own moral codes unique to each particular narrative. The audience does not find meaning through the story world's moral code alone, or solely through their own preexisting codes, but through the comparison or contrast between the two. Some stories present more perfect worlds with idealistic systems of morals that our own world should strive to emulate. Others present worlds with flaws like our own through which we may recognize the problems we face and find potential solutions. Yet others present corrupted or degraded worlds filled with consequences our own world should make an effort to avoid. Though the story world is not the real world, we learn about our real world by comparing it to an alternative.

Since story worlds are morally-relativistic, the definition of a "flaw" or "negative character trait" must be relative as well. In everyday usage, these terms come with cultural charges attached. If one says a person has a flaw or negative trait, this usually means the individual possesses a quality his or her culture finds undesirable. However, when it comes to the cold, neutral nature of story structure, cultural notions of rightness or wrongness are irrelevant. In screencraft, a "negative trait" means (and only means) a personal quality that interferes with the protagonist's ability to achieve the Story Goal. It is negative because it pushes the protagonist in the wrong direction. In some stories, such traits may be qualities the audience would otherwise find desirable. In *The Godfather*, Michael Corleone is originally hampered by the idealized notions of morality he acquired in college and the military. In *One Flew Over the Cuckoo's Nest*, R.P. McMurphy brings trouble upon himself for being a free-thinking individualist. Though the audience may find reason to approve of these traits, they nevertheless run counter to the protagonist's chances of success. This makes them detrimental, and thus must be abandoned. The reverse can also be true. In some stories, the protagonist demonstrates qualities the audience finds socially undesirable, but unless these qualities directly impede the protagonist's pursuit of victory, they are not negative traits. To the contrary, these traits may help the protagonist, making them positive in nature. What is "positive" and what is "negative" is ultimately determined by the morally relativistic system of the story world. This means behavior that leads to victory in one story may lead to failure in another, regardless of the audience's opinions of virtue or vice.

However, none of this is meant to suggest that story worlds are morally bankrupt or lacking any kind of guiding ethos. To the contrary, the coincidences, surprise occurrences, and twists of fate present in every story indeed suggest some higher power in control of its universe. Story worlds can essentially be considered conscious things. They have a mind and a will that oversees all events, handing out reward and punishment based upon some preexisting ethical nature. To form an analogy, each story world can be thought of as a unique, self-contained ecosystem operating by its own set of rules. Primitive societies often believed that natural ecosystems such as forests or mountains contained a deity or collective spirit that acted to maintain balance and order. Those who respected this spirit or deity prospered. Those who did not were punished. A samesuch consciousness presides over a story world. This consciousness sees all and controls all. It exists to ensure that a natural order is maintained. To live and prosper, characters must learn to abide by the will of their story world. Those who obey its rules are rewarded. Those who act contrary to its rules are punished.

On its most basic level, the protagonist's journey lies in the struggle to identify the rules of his or her story world. Victory or failure is then determined by whether the protagonist conforms his or her behavior to these expectations. If the protagonist agrees to behave as the world wishes, he or she is rewarded. If the protagonist rejects or fails to recognize the world's wishes, he or she is punished. Though on its surface a story may seem to be about a character versus a character, a character versus an environment, or a character versus a society, at its core every story is really about the protagonist's struggle to resolve his or her personal nature with the nature of the story world.

The particular nature of each story world is most easily understood through a concept we will call WORLD ALIGNMENT. As we shall see, the structural pattern that unifies all traditionally-told cinematic narratives; whether they be Celebratory, Cautionary, Tragic, or Cynical; ultimately comes down to a very simple thing: How the story world is aligned, and how the protagonist's actions stand in relation to it.

## WORLD ALIGNMENT

The idea of the story world as a conscious entity is not such a fanciful notion. After all, the consciousness of the story world is actually the consciousness of the storyteller. The storyteller created this world to communicate his or her ideas and beliefs. Furthermore, the storyteller imposes control over events and outcomes for the purpose of expressing those ideas and beliefs. Yet effective communication requires that the story's message be clearly received and easily understood. To avoid confusion or ambiguity, the storyteller creates a simplified world that operates by an ethical framework far more basic than that found in reality. This is once again accomplished by relying on the simple duality of THEME versus ANTI-THEME.

To review, a story's Thematic Argument pits a certain moral, social, or behavioral value against its exact opposite. Compassion versus indifference. Individuality versus conformity. Romanticism versus pragmatism. Through narrative conflict, characters engage in a symbolic battle to decide which value is greater. Yet little do characters know that the story world is not a neutral party in this fight. As the consciousness which oversees all things, the story world has itself chosen a side. By its very nature, the story world has committed itself to supporting and rewarding behaviors that reflect one side of the Thematic Argument, while ignoring, rejecting, or punishing the behaviors found on the other.

The story world does not merely endorse this particular value. This value forms the core of the story world's entire ethical system. All story actions are evaluated in terms of this one value and granted outcomes accordingly. Therefore, the supported thematic ideal can be considered the *controlling value* of the story's universe—the single "truth" by which all things are judged. Characters who embrace the controlling value find themselves supported and empowered by their world. They are *correctly aligned* with the forces of their universe and are thus pushed forward by its natural current. Characters who embrace the opposing value choose to fight against the story world. They are *misaligned* with the forces of their universe and act contrary to its nature. While these characters may keep themselves afloat for a while, they are eventually overpowered by the world and meet their demise.

Therefore, we see there really is a correct side to the Thematic Argument and an incorrect side. Those on the same side as their story world will always win and those on the opposing side will always lose. In previous discussions on the Thematic Argument, it was left intentionally unclear as to which of the two opposing values should be officially labeled the "theme" and which should be labeled the "anti-theme." One may have assumed that the "theme" always denotes the more socially-constructive of the two values and the "anti-theme" the less desirable of the pair. However, this is not always so. In the Thematic Argument, the "theme" always implies the value supported by the story world and the "anti-theme" the value it opposes. This means the labels of theme and anti-theme have nothing to do with good and bad or right and wrong. Because of the principle of moral relativism, some story worlds promote a controlling value the audience indeed considers good, righteous, or socially-uplifting, while others promote a value the audience considers harmful or wrong. This is essentially the difference between the "Worlds of Light" of the Celebratory and Cautionary narratives and the "Worlds of Darkness" of the Tragic and Cynical. Regardless of the case, the world-supported value is always the story's "theme," as it will always decide the protagonist's ultimate success or failure, irrespective of whether the audience approves of this value or not.

No matter what kind of value the story world supports, two unbreakable rules govern the course of the narrative. First, *the story world always wins.* The story world is all-powerful and all-knowing. Nothing can be done to defeat it. Its controlling value exists as an unquestionable truth that must be accepted or else. Anyone who rebels against the controlling value may achieve some small victories or momentary gains, but this is like trying to defy gravity. With time, everything will be pulled back into its proper place. No matter what actions characters may take throughout the course of the narrative, events will always be resolved in a matter that reverts the world back to its natural order. A story ends with the controlling value once again reigning supreme and all those who have challenged it resigned to defeat.

Yet despite all the power of the story world, it cannot force characters to do anything they do not wish. In this we find the second rule: *Characters continue to possess free will.** Though surrounded by intense pressures, characters are still allowed to think and act however they please. While the story world can manipulate events in an attempt to push characters in one direction or the other, it is ultimately up to the character to decide which value to embrace. Proverbially speaking, the story world can lead a character to water, but it cannot make it drink. If the character should recognize the world's controlling value and align him or herself with it, that is the character's choice. If the character should reject the controlling value, that is the character's choice as well. In other words, characters hold their fates in their own hands. Choose wisely and the path leads to salvation. Choose otherwise and it leads to ruin.

Yet if the story world is indeed all-powerful, one may wonder why some stories begin with their worlds overrun by the opposing anti-thematic value. For instance, the world of *Star Wars* supposedly supports and rewards those who serve the altruistic ideals of the Force, yet the Empire has been allowed to enslave the galaxy through tyranny and oppression. Likewise, the world of *The Shawshank Redemption* rewards those who preserve the light of humanity (see Chapter 1-6), yet begins as a place where such light has been all but snuffed out. If the story world is all-powerful, should it not have prevented this from ever happening? How did these supposedly-virtuous worlds become so corrupted?

---

* This does not contradict a statement found in Chapter 8 of *Screenwriting Down to the Atoms*. The statement in *Atoms* refers to methods used to force characters to take actions necessary to advance the plot. Here, free will refers to the character's continued ability to make personal decisions and form his or her own beliefs. While plot events may force characters to take actions they do not wish, a character's internal will remains under his or her control.

Philosophically, such questions are very similar to what is known as the "Question of Evil." The Question of Evil asks, if God is benevolent and all-powerful, why does evil still exist? The most common answer relates just as much to story as it does to theology. Human beings have been given the gift of free will. They can choose their own paths and make their own decisions. However, this gift comes at a price. Because human beings possess a capacity for both right and wrong, they cannot be granted salvation automatically. Instead, salvation must be earned. Free will turns life into a test. People have the ability to do wrong, but must resist the temptation and remain on a morally-righteous path. Unfortunately, many individuals abuse free will by choosing to act in an immoral manner. Therefore, evil exists. Yet this does not mean the world is without justice for evildoers. The wicked will eventually be punished. Not with the fleeting, material kind of punishment found on earth, but one which is cosmic and eternal. Judgment eventually comes to all, but it waits until the proper time. Until then, individuals are given the opportunity to correct their ways before the curtain falls.

Likewise in story, a world's inhabitants possess the free will to either accept or reject the controlling value. When rejection becomes rampant or widespread, the world falls into disrepair and its opposing value seizes control. The evil Empire of *Star Wars* has been allowed to thrive only because the inhabitants of its universe have forgotten the guiding values of The Force. Shawshank Prison has become such a dehumanizing place only because its inhabitants have forgotten or given up on their light of humanity. Yet though these worlds have become befouled on their surface, this does not mean their core natures have changed. The controlling value still lies dormant underneath, waiting to reassert itself and revert the world back to its natural order. Such scenarios are quite common in stories of the Celebratory type (*The Matrix, Back to the Future, The Bourne Identity* to name a few more). When these stories call their protagonists to action, the story world essentially asks the character to become the tool through which the controlling value is restored. Yet once again we encounter the problem of free will. Will the protagonist accept this call? Or will the protagonist reject this responsibility and succumb to his or her flaws?

World alignment provides the key that unites the Story Spine, Character Arc, and Thematic Argument into a single unified structure. Every protagonist begins the story "flawed." This means he or she possesses attitudes or behaviors misaligned with the story world's controlling value. Because the protagonist behaves in ways antithetical to the world's nature, his or her actions fail to achieve positive results. As previously stated, though the protagonist may face many physical obstacles and challenges, success or failure is ultimately dependent upon the character's ability to recognize the true nature of his or her world and then alter his or her behavior in accordance to its demands. The Character Arc therefore dramatizes a process of *realignment*. To succeed, the protagonist must abandon all antithetical behaviors and fully adopt the story world's controlling value. This empowers the protagonist. Rather than continue to fight against the story world's natural current, he or she now moves with it. By embracing the controlling value, the protagonist embraces the source of the world's power and achieves victory through it. Protagonists who fail to realign continue to defy the story world's natural order and are punished for it. Like a ship sailing directly against a storm, they are eventually overcome by the forces of their world, pulled under, and drowned.

## IN CONCLUSION: THE BASIC UNIFIED NARRATIVE STRUCTURE

The process just described illustrates the basic model by which virtually every successful Hollywood or American Independent feature film operates.* Whether it be Celebratory, Cautionary, Tragic, or Cynical, every traditionally-told cinematic narrative unfolds by this simple form. This chapter concludes by describing this process in more detail, incorporating the previously-

---

* Two important qualifiers have been added to this statement. The first is "successful." While both systems often produce films that fail to properly abide by the basic unified structure, these films tend to find far less success with audiences. Thus, they provide the exceptions that prove the rule. The second is "virtually." The basic unified structure is not fully universal to Hollywood and American Independent filmmaking, but only near-universal. There are rare cases of successful films that operate by alternative structures. These alternatives will be discussed in Chapter 1-7.

established principles of the Story Spine, Character Arc, and Thematic Argument to reveal how screencraft's many structural elements converge to create a unified narrative form.

Every story begins with two things: the creation of a story world and the selection of a protagonist.

The story world is essentially a conscious thing. At the heart of this consciousness is a controlling moral, ethical, or social value by which it evaluates all things. This world is at harmony when its inhabitants obey this controlling value. Problems arise when behaviors contradict it. Conflicts inevitably form between those who act according to the controlling value and those who defy it. These conflicts become not only the source of the plot's physical action, but the substance of the story's Thematic Argument.

The protagonist is chosen specifically because he or she currently stands misaligned with the story world's controlling value. The protagonist lives by a flawed set of beliefs that cause him or her to think and act in ways antithetical to the world's nature. Because of this misalignment, the protagonist struggles with life in some shape or form. His or her inaccurate view of the world has prevented positive personal development, blocking the protagonist from an important emotional or psychological Need. The protagonist cannot achieve this Internal Need until he or she realigns with the story world by adopting the proper attitudes and behaviors. Unfortunately, the protagonist is unaware of his or her misalignment and therefore takes no action to pursue change voluntarily. In response, the story world causes physical events to arise intended to expose and then challenge the protagonist's misalignment in an effort to motivate personal change.

Unexpected events throw the protagonist into a physical conflict as both a motivation and a test. Confronted by a Story Problem and a Story Goal, the protagonist is forced to take action in search of a positive resolution. Yet due to his or her misalignment, the protagonist begins this quest using methods which the story world does not endorse or approve. Rather than ameliorate the situation, the protagonist's actions rub the world the wrong way, creating more problems and aggravating the situation further.

Eventually, the protagonist's misaligned actions accumulate to create a major complication (AKA the monster moment). Basically, the story world is fed up with the protagonist's behavior and manipulates events further to force the protagonist to make a Crucial Decision. Faced with a far more threatening situation of his or her own making, the protagonist can either recognize that his or her actions are misaligned and reform his or her behavior, or the protagonist can defy the story world by rejecting realignment.

Here, the unified structure splits into two possible paths. In the first, the protagonist chooses to convert (found in the Celebratory and Cynical narratives). Rather than continue to fight against the current, the protagonist switches polarity by adopting new methods far more in line with the story world's controlling value. This change benefits the protagonist, ultimately rewarding him or her with victory. In the second, the protagonist rejects the controlling value and willfully chooses to remain misaligned (found in the Cautionary and Tragic narratives). With this decision, the protagonist essentially declares war upon the story world and the value it supports. However, this is a fool's path. The story world is all-powerful and always wins. Therefore, this choice can only lead to failure.

While the protagonists of Celebratory and Cynical narratives do initially choose to realign themselves with the controlling value, this conversion typically begins far more in word than in deed. The protagonist foolishly retains some of his or her misaligned attitudes, behaviors, or beliefs. In other words, the protagonist only partially converts. Because of this, old behaviors return to undermine the protagonist's new efforts, causing troubles to escalate. This eventually leads to a crisis event in which the protagonist's failure at full realignment threatens him or her with irreversible defeat. In the following moment of truth, the protagonist realizes success is impossible unless he or she offers full surrender to the controlling value. The story world demands nothing less. So, the protagonist fully abandons his or her former antithetical attitudes, behaviors, and beliefs and experiences a MOMENT OF FULL CONVERSION.

Now completely aligned with the story world, the protagonist implements the power of the controlling value with actions that overcome all remaining obstacles, defeat all sources of conflict, and resolve the Story Problem. With this victory, balance and order are restored to the story world. The controlling value reigns supreme, proving it to be the superior thematic ideal. Thanks to realignment, the protagonist is rewarded with not only physical victory, but also the Internal Need.

Cautionary and Tragic protagonists follow a much different road. By rejecting the controlling value, the protagonist permanently aligns him or herself against the story world. The protagonist then escalates his or her misaligned behavior out of a belief that he or she can defeat the story world through its means. However, the story world cannot be defeated by these means or any other. By trying to defeat the undefeatable, the protagonist only entrenches him or herself in an ever-deepening hole. Yet while the cause of failure may now be obvious, the protagonist refuses to see the light. The Fatal Flaw has grown from a preoccupation to a full-blown obsession, warping the protagonist's judgment beyond all reason. With every setback, the protagonist only intensifies his or her misalignment more and more.

This inevitably leads to a different kind of crisis event. Faced with the consequences of his or her actions, the protagonist receives one last opportunity to repent his or her misguided ways and convert to the proper alignment. Yet the protagonist rejects this opportunity as well, and responds to the crisis with an action so misaligned that it seals his or her irreversible doom. We will call this event the NAIL IN THE COFFIN.

With the Nail in the Coffin, the protagonist passes a point of no return, initiating a downward spiral of events that eventually leads to a crushing defeat. With the troublemaker eliminated, the story world reverts back to its natural order with the controlling value once again ruling all. The story world always wins in the end. Swimming against its current causes the protagonist to drown.

# THE UNIFIED NARRATIVE STRUCTURE

A story begins with a world that operates by an ethical framework orientated around a controlling value. At the start, the world may function as intended or may have become warped, corrupted, or put under threat by forces opposing this value.

A protagonist is chosen. This protagonist is flawed due to behaviors, attitudes, or beliefs that run contrary to the controlling value. This misalignment prevents the protagonist from achieving an Internal Need he or she requires for a happier, more prosperous life.

INCITING INCIDENT

A Story Problem enters the protagonist's life, thrusting him or her into a physical conflict. To overcome this conflict, the protagonist must take willful action in pursuit of a Story Goal.

The protagonist pursues the Story Goal through his or her accustomed behavior. Since these behaviors run counter to the story world's nature, the protagonist's actions aggravate the situation and cause new problems to arise.

(CONT'D)

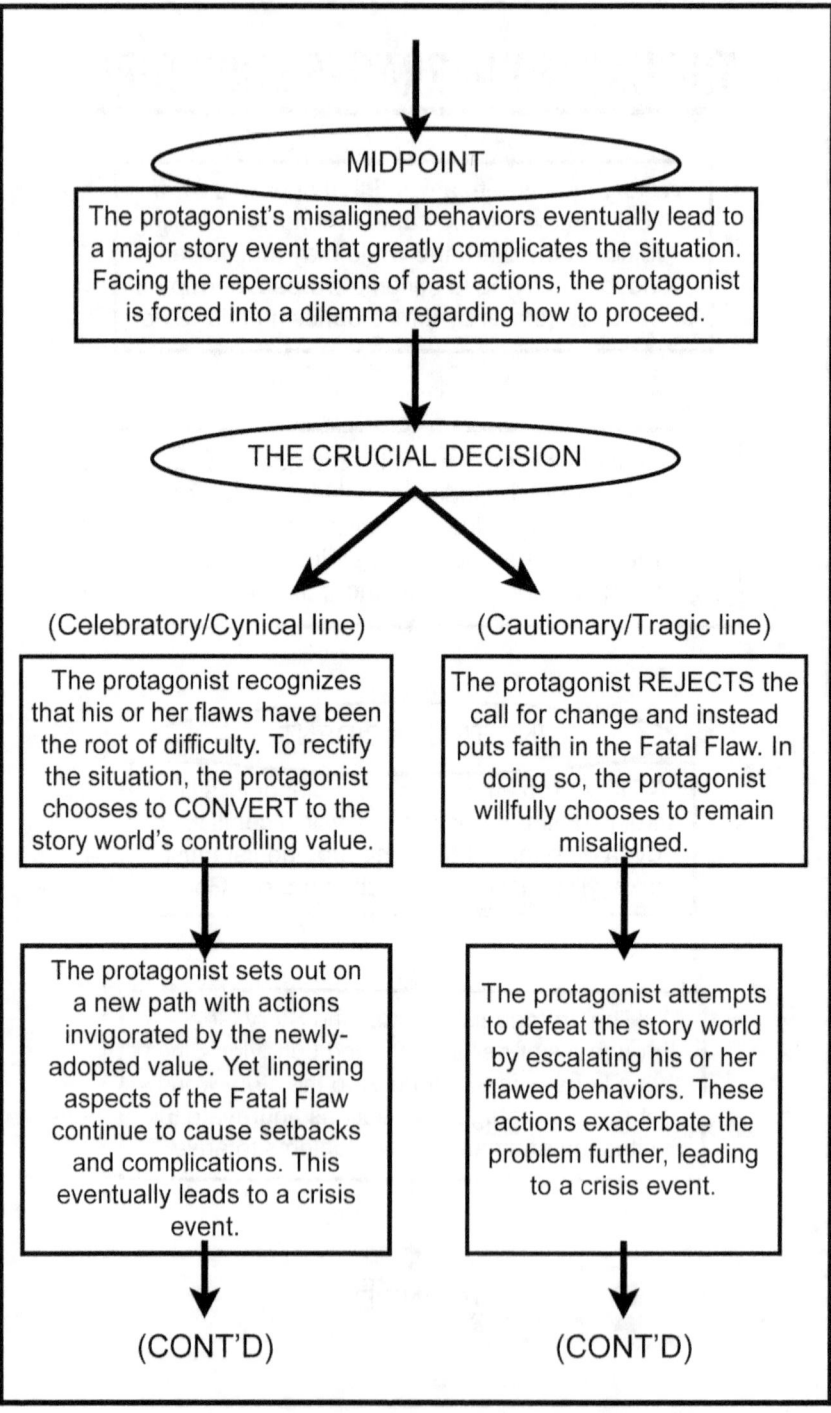

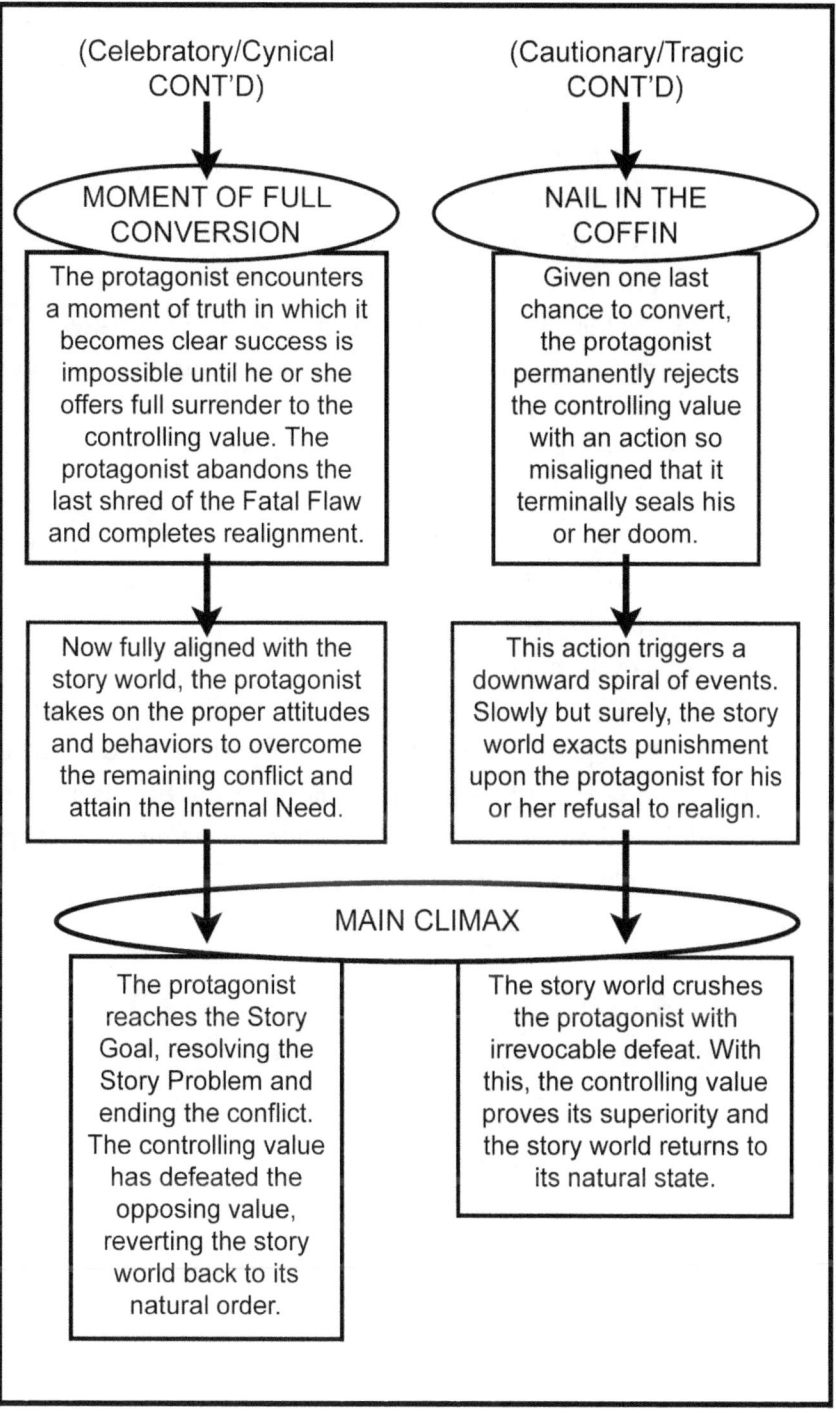

In conclusion, all four types of narrative; Celebratory, Cautionary, Tragic, and Cynical; follow the exact same structure. The only difference is which path the protagonist chooses at the moment of Crucial Decision. All other disparities between narrative types arise from the audience's interpretation of the story's controlling value. Since all traditionally-told Hollywood or American Independent films fit into one of the four narrative types, it must be concluded that every successful film of traditional form produced by these systems follows this singular unified structure. With its seamless unification of plot, character, and theme, this structure has provided Hollywood and American Independent filmmaking the ability to tell a never-ending variety of stories in ways that continually fulfill the technical requirements of the medium, the psychological needs of the audience, and the artistic ambitions of the storyteller all at the same time. Hence, this structure is the source of Hollywood and American Independent cinema's enduring strength and vitality and the reason why the magic of movies has yet to wane after over a hundred years.

To give this model further substance and specificity, the following chapter has selected twelve highly-successful films, three of each narrative type, for individual analysis. Ranging from popular favorites to Oscar recipients, every one of these films provides a clear example of the unified narrative structure despite obvious differences in genre, content, style, or tone.

# CHAPTER 1-6
# A CLOSER LOOK: THE SAMPLE FILMS

First comes the theory, now comes the practice. The previous chapters have established the principles by which the unified narrative structure operates. This chapter illustrates those principles in action.

The purpose of this chapter is twofold. The first is to prove that the unified structure is not only present, but nearly ubiquitous to all* successful Hollywood and American Independent stories regardless of genre, content, tone, or thematic intent.

The second purpose is to prove that the structure is truly effective. The principles of the unified structure have shaped these films' narratives into a form that communicates as well as entertains. It combines the structures of plot, character, and theme into a seamlessly-flowing and dramatically satisfying whole that fulfills all three levels of the audience's psychological needs. Meanwhile, the unified structure communicates an ideological message by uniting all story elements under a philosophical dualism. By establishing a controlling value and then dramatizing the consequences of accepting or rejecting that value, the story fulfills its artistic purpose of ideological communication through dramatic conflict.

* See Chapter 1-7 for information on films that use alternative structures.

For best results, readers should be familiar with these twelve films before proceeding. If you have not yet seen all of them, I suggest you do so now. After completing this chapter, I encourage readers to take a look at other successful films to observe how the unified narrative structure operates within them as well.

# THE CELEBRATORY

To review, Celebratory narratives promote a certain cultural or social value by presenting that value as a key to personal success. The protagonist begins the story exhibiting behaviors contrary to this value. Eventually, setbacks and failures cause the protagonist to recognize his or her behavioral misalignment and accept a path to personal change. The protagonist achieves victory by realigning with the story world's controlling value. By comparing the protagonist's struggles before conversion to the far greater success achieved afterward, the story proves the worth of the controlling value and encourages the audience to adopt it into their own lives.

## *Back to the Future*

Viewed purely in terms of its premise, *Back to the Future* is a fantasy-adventure about time travel. However, when evaluated as a whole, the film can be more accurately described as a lesson on the importance of taking responsibility for one's own future. *Back to the Future* is an excellent example of using the properties of storytelling to transform abstract meaning into physical form. Using a play on words, an ideological concept (persons should take responsibility for their futures) is turned literal (a young man is trapped in the past, a setting which forces him to take responsibility for how his current actions influence future events). In this way, the story's ideological message is delivered through a physically-observable conflict.

Consistent with cinematic structure, *Back to the Future* selects a protagonist who, due to his Fatal Flaw, seems to be the person least likely to overcome the Story Problem. Marty McFly is a reckless and irresponsible teenager. He gives no thought to his future and rarely stops to consider the possible consequences of his actions. If he remains this way, Marty will likely end up just like his father George. George did not take responsibility for his future either. As a result, he has nothing to show for his life but a pathetic job, a dissatisfied wife, and a bully he has not been able to shake since high school. Yet unlike Marty, George did not fail due to recklessness. He failed due to cowardice and passivity. George was afraid to take control of his future and thus allowed the future to control him. Yet a third variation on this flaw is found in Marty's mentor Doc Brown. Doc suffers from a fatalist view of the future. He believes what happens must happen and no one should do anything to change it, even in cases of life or death. Marty, George, and Doc all share the same Internal Need. They must accept responsibility for their own futures. Yet each character possesses a different variation on the type of flawed attitudes that may block one from this Need. With these three characters, the story lays the groundwork for its Thematic Argument even before the adventure begins. The story world is aligned to reward those who take responsibility for their futures and punish those who do not.

Since Marty, George, and Doc all begin the story misaligned with the controlling value, the storyteller-god must manipulate events to teach them all a swift and brutal lesson. So, the plot imposes an extreme twist of fate that traps Marty thirty years in the past. The storyteller-god does this as both a challenge and a test. Every action Marty takes in 1955 has a ripple effect that will alter his future in 1985. This means Marty must learn to think through the potential consequences of his actions before committing them. Otherwise, he will literally destroy his future and never find his way home.

Yet Marty does very poorly at this test at first. In no time at all, Marty exacerbates the Story Problem through his natural recklessness and impulsivity. Marty alters history by pushing his future father George out of the path of a speeding car. This inadvertently prevents George from meeting Marty's mother Lorraine, which in turn prevents them from falling in love and eventually conceiving Marty. In other words, Marty's misaligned behaviors unwittingly transform the situation into something far worse.

Marty is now not only stuck in the past, but has created a temporal paradox that threatens to wipe him out of existence. When this mistake is discovered, Doc convinces Marty that he must change his behavior if he is ever to return home. He must take responsibility for his future (quite literally) by correcting his past errors through prudent, well thought-out actions. With this, Marty accepts the story world's controlling value and commits himself to a path of change.

Unfortunately, Marty's old habits are hard to shake. Time and again, Marty backslides into recklessness and impulsivity, creating further stumbling blocks of his own making. With each mistake, Marty must rededicate himself to the controlling value, slowly shedding his old ways and growing into a more responsible individual. In doing so, Marty survives his crisis event at the end of the second act, puts his world back in the right order, and is able to face the final challenge of returning home.

The connections between plot, character, and theme are made even clearer by how Marty's process of transformation leads George and Doc to embrace the controlling value as well. For Marty to overcome his mistakes, he must first teach George to abandon his passivity and take charge of his own life. In the same way, Doc's adventure with Marty gives Doc a glimpse of his own future, causing Doc to become more flexible in his fatalism. All three characters are rewarded for their realignment. Marty is able to return to 1985. Doc survives the attack from the Libyan radicals. George is now a successful man with a happy marriage and a bully who will never mess with him again. With this conclusion, *Back to the Future* celebrates the value of personal responsibility. The story proves this value to be not only a key to success, but a source of endless rewards.

## Rocky

Everyone in *Rocky* wants the same thing. Rocky Balboa wants it. Adrian wants it. Mick and Paulie want it. Even Apollo Creed wants it. They all want a feeling of self-worth. They crave some sense of value that others will recognize and respect. Unfortunately, in this story's hard scrabble, dog-eat-dog world, most people try to get their worth by stealing it from others.

*Rocky* opens with its protagonist mercilessly jeered by a roomful of strangers. It makes no difference that Rocky wins this opening fight. It makes no difference that Rocky gets his face bashed in for their entertainment. They boo him anyway because tearing someone down makes them feel better about themselves. These people are takers. *Rocky*'s world is filled with takers. But as the story's Thematic Argument later proves, true self-worth comes not to those who take, but those who learn to give.

Despite his tough exterior, Rocky Balboa is an emotionally sensitive guy. Because of this, Rocky has come to believe all the takers who tell him he is nothing but a loser. This creates a self-defeating paradigm that blocks Rocky from his Internal Need. Rocky cannot commit the actions necessary to gain self-worth until he abandons the notion that he does not deserve it. Adrian begins in the same situation. She has been left to believe she is worthless, largely by her brother Paulie, a man who achieves his own feeling of worth by stealing it from his sister. It is not certain what initially attracts Rocky to Adrian, but it is clear that Rocky's romantic pursuit is motivated by his Internal Need. If he can get Adrian to love him, he will feel a greater sense of worth. Rocky first attempts to woo Adrian with dumb jokes and non-stop talk about his boxing career. He is saying "I have value. Please recognize it." Yet Rocky makes little progress with this approach. Adrian has come to believe that no man could find her desirable, so Rocky's attentions must be some kind of joke. Fortunately, Rocky overcomes this obstacle by switching tactics. Instead of asking Adrian to recognize his value, he first shows that he recognizes value in her. By first giving worth, Rocky eventually receives it himself, forming a mutually-supportive bond between the two characters.

Though Rocky's romance of Adrian serves only as a prelude to the story proper, it establishes the thematic pattern by which the narrative unfolds. *Rocky* is filled with characters who seem to shout "I have value, please recognize it," yet initially go about this pursuit in the wrong way. As the story progresses, a thematic divide develops between those who try to steal self-worth from others and those who earn worth by first *giving it away*. The story rewards those who learn to give. Those who do not are left to struggle all alone.

However, this behavior does not come easily to those in Rocky's world. As always, the plot must intervene with a dramatic situation contrived to motivate characters towards the proper personal change. Rocky is selected from obscurity to fight Heavyweight Champion Apollo Creed. Though this gives Rocky the opportunity of a lifetime, Rocky initially resists. Because of his Flaw, Rocky does not believe he deserves the opportunity. Furthermore, he knows this is not the magnanimous gesture Apollo promotes it to be. Apollo is a taker, not a giver. He wants to increase his popularity by embarrassing a small-timer. Rocky does not ultimately accept the offer because he thinks he can win. He accepts because, as someone destined to become a broken-down loser, he might as well earn a little money along the way. Of course, with this flawed attitude, Rocky is sure to end up thoroughly defeated.

However, something interesting happens once Rocky accepts. All the former takers in Rocky's life suddenly want to give. Mick wants to help. Paulie wants to help. Even loan shark Tony Gazzo wants to help. Yet Rocky resists. He is sure they do not really believe in him. Like Adrian before, Rocky does not see these offers as genuine because he remains certain of his own lack of worth. Because his Flaw holds fast, Rocky rejects this help and remains destined to fail.

Rocky's fortunes begin to turn at the Midpoint as characters one by one learn to give worth in a way that Rocky can accept as honest and genuine. Receiving true expressions of worth challenges Rocky's flawed perception of self and begins his personal transformation. Mick is the first character to convert. Mick is a broken-down hasbeen who sees Rocky's fight as a way to regain the worth he has lost. However, Mick initially goes about this in a misguided way. His offer to train Rocky is insulting and boastful. Rocky, resentful of all the times Mick has denied him worth in the past, leans on his flawed attitudes and creates what amounts to his monster moment by rejecting and humiliating Mick. Yet as Mick leaves, Rocky quickly realizes he faces a Crucial Decision. Rocky knows he is doomed against Creed all alone. Mick's help may be his only hope. Rocky knows that Mick deserves the value he asks for. Yet Rocky's Fatal Flaw makes him bitter and angry. He wants to get back at those who have made him feel worthless in the past.

Fortunately, Rocky chooses to put his bruised ego aside and give Mick a chance. With this, both characters accept the controlling value. They both give worth to each other and both receive worth in return. Like with Adrian before, a mutually-supportive relationship forms between Rocky and Mick, allowing Rocky to grow stronger, smarter, and more capable of achieving his Story Goal.

Paulie is a far later holdout. Throughout the story, Paulie's only wish is that someone recognize his value, but he goes about this by being a bully. He of course gets no reward from such actions. It is not until Paulie makes an effort to give that he starts to receive something in return.

Yet, true to the Celebratory structure, Rocky's Fatal Flaw continues to linger. Despite the love and support he has received from others, despite the strength and skill he has gained from their help, Rocky remains certain that he is just a pretender. He will never be able to defeat Apollo and will never be able to prove his worth to the world. Though he has given worth to others, Rocky still denies it to himself. Thus, Rocky remains partially misaligned and destined to fail. This failure to relinquish self-doubt leads Rocky to a crisis moment at the end of Act 2B. Faced with what seems to be certain defeat, Rocky searches his soul for a solution. While it may indeed be impossible to beat Apollo, Rocky comes to the realization that he has grown to a point where he may be able to go the distance against him. No fighter has ever lasted fifteen rounds against Apollo Creed, making it a great accomplishment the world cannot deny. With this newfound confidence in his abilities, Rocky sheds the self-doubt that has held him back. He *is* good enough and he can prove it to all those who formerly made him believe otherwise. By finally giving worth to himself, Rocky fully embraces the controlling value and attains full conversion, allowing him to enter the story's final stage with the attitudes and behaviors necessary for success.

In the final battle, Rocky is rewarded for his transformation. While the taker Apollo continues to treat Rocky like a joke, Rocky shocks him and the world by staying on his feet until the last bell, earning a recognition of worth that no one, including himself, can ever deny. Yet Rocky did not achieve this victory on his own. It would have been impossible without the love and support he received from others. Rocky's success was a collective effort, making this end a victory for every character who embraced the controlling value. With this resolution, *Rocky* delivers its final message: When it comes to happiness, we are all in it together. Stealing worth from others only hurts ourselves. Yet when individuals learn to support each other with mutual love and respect, the rising tide lifts all ships, granting everyone a better and more satisfying existence.

## The Shawshank Redemption

There are few places on earth more dehumanizing than prison. In such places, men are treated like animals, making it easy to forget the hopes and joys that allow one to feel like a human being. It is in this kind of dark and hopeless environment that *The Shawshank Redemption* finds the extreme contrasts necessary to show us what being human really means.

*The Shawshank Redemption* presents the battle of a man striving to retain his humanity in an inhumane place against forces who wish to snuff it out. At a certain point, the film quotes John 8:12, "He that followeth me shall have the light of life." This line echoes the story's core thematic concept, with the "light of life" referring to the spark of humanity that gives life its sense of joy, hope, and meaning. Protagonist Andy Dufresne is then told "Salvation lies within." This also has a thematic double-meaning. *Shawshank*'s narrative intends to prove that in the darkest of times, personal salvation can only come by holding onto the light of life within oneself. As the story unfolds, the story world rewards those who nurture their light, does nothing for those who ignore it, and ultimately brings punishment to those who try to snuff it out in others.

Yet as usual, Andy Dufresne fails to recognize or appreciate this thematic value when his story begins. Andy starts as a deeply misaligned individual. We first meet him with a gun in his hand, waiting to confront his wife and her lover. Andy has become an "icy and remorseless character" who has not only allowed his own light to dim, but feels he has the right to extinguish it in others. To force Andy to transform into a more virtuous individual, the storyteller-god orchestrates a cruel twist of fate that sends Andy to

Shawshank Prison, trapping him in a situation where he must either find and embrace his light of life or wither away and die.

Facing the reality that he will be in prison for the rest of his life, Andy concedes he "better get busy living, or get busy dying." Andy's first actions are fairly simple. He asks Red for a rockhammer so he may continue a hobby he had on the outside. This will help him feel like he is still human. While not much, this initial resolve leads to a later event where Andy takes a bigger risk with Captain Hadley to bring a brief spark of life back into Shawshank's walls. To Andy's surprise, the story world rewards him for this. First, his tormentors the Sisters are eradicated. Then Andy is given a special position that recognizes his value as an individual. These rewards teach Andy the power of the controlling value, compelling him to take on the role of its champion. Andy then launches a series of actions which make Shawshank a place where hope and humanity can continue to exist.

Yet like all protagonists, Andy is hampered by a Fatal Flaw. As a highly-educated former banker, Andy has a sizable ego. Furthermore, Andy's innocence makes him arrogant. Andy acts as if he is above the world that imprisons him, at times above Warden Norton himself. This Flaw gets Andy in trouble at various times. It nearly gets him thrown off the roof by Captain Hadley. It gets him a beating of a lifetime from the Sisters. It gets him two weeks in solitary confinement for locking himself in Norton's office. By embracing the controlling value but neglecting to abandon his Flaw, Andy plays a dangerous game that threatens to draw him off the righteous path.

In the story's second half, Andy allows Warden Norton to exploit his ego and pervert his virtuous ambitions. Andy becomes entangled in Norton's criminal scheme, a path that leads to his downfall when it blocks his one and only chance to prove his innocence. In response, Andy foolishly challenges Warden Norton. This arrogance becomes Andy's undoing. Norton crushes Andy with all of his power, creating a crisis event that nearly destroys Andy completely.

With things now at their darkest and most hopeless, Andy encounters his moment of truth. He realizes his ego means nothing in this place. Clinging to it has only caused him to lose his way. Humbled into abandoning his

Flaw, Andy realizes that if he is to truly serve the controlling value, he cannot continue to compromise or coexist with the forces of dehumanization. To the contrary, he must take it upon himself to eliminate them.

Empowered by his moment of Full Conversion, Andy escapes Shawshank Prison and exposes its brutality and corruption to the world. As the sampler on Norton's wall states, "His justice cometh, and that right soon." Andy's actions allow the story world's natural alignment to reassert itself and bring swift punishment to its violators. Captain Hadley is arrested. Warden Norton commits suicide. Andy, on the other hand, is rewarded with a new life in paradise; and Red, by learning to reignite his own light of life, is allowed to join him.

# THE CAUTIONARY

As previously stated, Cautionary narratives present story worlds designed to support and reward values the viewing audience considers virtuous or socially-constructive. However, the protagonists of these stories refuse to embrace or in many cases even recognize these values due to a preoccupation with their Fatal Flaw. Since the protagonist rejects the controlling value, the story world has no choice but to punish the protagonist with defeat. Cautionary narratives promote socially-supported values by showing the consequences of their rejection.

## *Raging Bull*

*Raging Bull* tells the story of middleweight boxer Jake "Raging Bull" La Motta. The nickname is appropriate, as La Motta is one of the most bull-headed protagonists ever put on screen. Jake behaves like an animal. He is an angry brute who gives nothing but shameful treatment to those who love and support him. However, this behavior is all a smoke screen to hide Jake's Fatal Flaw. Jake suffers from an extreme insecurity. He feels he stands alone against the world and refuses to trust anyone, whether it be his brother Joey, his wife Vickie, or the neighborhood friends and supporters who just want the best for him. This insecurity stands at the root of all Jake's negative traits, from his irrational jealousy to his stupid, self-defeating pride. If Jake is to succeed, he must learn to trust others. Trust is the story world's controlling value. However, as the story unfolds, Jake grows so obsessed with his insecurity that realignment never occurs, leading him to a sad and lonely end.

Just as in *Rocky,* the world of boxing provides only a background for Jake's far more personal struggle. Jake's Flaw has made him unhappy and dissatisfied with life. He initially tries to fill this lack with the pursuit of fifteen year-old Vickie (despite Jake already being married). However, unlike the romance found in *Rocky,* this is a misguided pursuit stemming from Jake's Fatal Flaw. Jake does not pursue Vickie out of love. This beautiful woman is a trophy to him. Jake believes possessing her will assuage his insecurity. However, marrying Vickie only worsens Jake's insecurity. Because he cannot trust anyone, Jake feels he must jealously defend Vickie as if she were a championship belt. Jake sabotages what could be a happy marriage with flawed, irrational behavior.

Such actions lead Jake to a moment of Crucial Decision at the story's Midpoint. Vickie has just inflamed Jake's insecurity by idly mentioning his next opponent is "good-looking." Now, Jake watches Vickie and Joey act a little too friendly towards acquaintances Jake mistrusts. With this, Jake encounters a dilemma. He can either decide to trust that Vickie will stay loyal and that Joey will do what is best for him, or he can reject this notion and indulge his Fatal Flaw. Jake chooses the latter. He rejects the controlling value and instead attempts to solve his problems by escalating his pride and jealousy.

By strengthening his attachment to the Fatal Flaw, Jake allows the Flaw to grow into an obsession. He becomes increasingly irrational and impossible to control. Pride turns into intractability. Jealousy turns into paranoia. This of course worsens Jake's problems. Joey and Vickie do their best to help, but rather than trust them, Jake leaps to the absurd conclusion that they are sleeping together. Given one last chance to curb his flawed behavior, Jake puts the Nail in his Coffin by brutally assaulting his brother, severing the relationship with the one person he should have trusted above all others. With this act, Jake seals his doom.

By irreversibly choosing insecurity over the controlling value of trust, Jake allows his Flaw to devour him whole, initiating a downward spiral of stupid and self-destructive acts that progressively destroy him in the final act. He loses his middleweight title in a brutal display of masochism. He pulls a stunt that lands him in jail. He destroys his most valued possession. Finally, he loses Vickie once and for all. Still, Jake does not learn anything from his mistakes. Because of this, he winds up sad and alone, a broken-down bum still trying to feed his insecurity as a third-rate entertainer for strangers who no longer care about him. By presenting the rise and fall of a man who could not overcome his flaws, *Raging Bull* warns viewers not to follow the same path or they will meet a similar fate.

## Amadeus

*Amadeus,* the fictionalized account of the rivalry between composer Antonio Salieri and Wolfgang Amadeus Mozart, is constructed as a dual-protagonist narrative. This means Salieri and Mozart are both protagonists, yet have spines opposed in such a way that each acts as the other's antagonist. This complicates the film's structure somewhat, but does not complicate the expression of theme. Salieri and Mozart are both guilty of the same sins: pride and jealousy. These sins lead to unhappy ends, for this story world is not aligned to support such petty and self-serving qualities, but rather their opposites: grace and humility. Grace is defined as the absolute and open-hearted acceptance of others, regardless of their virtues or flaws. Salieri meets his downfall by refusing to extend grace to Mozart (as well as grace to himself). Humility is an absence of pretension or self-importance. Mozart's massive ego continually rejects humility, and with it a path to salvation. Both of these failures come from pride and jealousy. Salieri and Mozart both meet their downfall by remaining aligned with the anti-theme.

Salieri begins the story a relatively satisfied man. His musical accomplishments have earned recognition and respect, granting him an enviable position in the royal court. Though Salieri pretends to carry himself with grace and humility, he is actually a very prideful person. This becomes apparent with the arrival of Mozart, a vulgar and arrogant youth with musical ability dwarfing Salieri's own. While a more humble and graceful individual would welcome Mozart with open arms, Salieri is inflamed by jealousy. Salieri has developed a flawed perception of the world in which he assumes talent to be a sign of God's love. If someone is more talented, it must mean that God loves that person more and him less. This of course is a false paradigm. Some people are simply more talented than others. One must have the grace to accept this. Yet Salieri perceives Mozart's arrival as a deliberate insult from God. Rather than learn the virtues of grace and humility, Salieri embraces his jealousy and attempts to expel Mozart from his life.

Mozart might have been able to withstand this opposition if it were not for his own Fatal Flaw. Past experiences with his father, another cold and graceless man, have made Mozart impudent towards authority figures and react arrogantly to any criticism. The audacity of Mozart's pride gains him nothing but enemies in the royal court. To Salieri, this justifies his feelings of contempt. Ignoring the true cause of his jealousy, Salieri sabotages Mozart's efforts under the pretext of teaching this vulgar youth a lesson.

These actions inevitably lead Salieri to a moral dilemma at the story's Midpoint. Despite the difficulties Salieri has inflicted upon Mozart, Mozart has composed "The Marriage of Figaro," a work of such beauty that it brings tears to Salieri's eyes. Forces of grace and humility urge Salieri to have a change of heart. At the same time, pride and jealousy urge Salieri to quash Mozart's greatness so that no one may ever see that Mozart is better than he. Salieri chooses pride and jealousy. With this Crucial Decision, Salieri permanently aligns himself against the controlling values of grace and humility and against his story world.

Again, Mozart might have been able to overcome Salieri's actions if Mozart did not also cling to his Fatal Flaw. Despite descending into poverty, Mozart refuses to correct his course with even an ounce of humility. Instead, Mozart intensifies his pride under the belief that he can defeat the world through the sheer power of his self-perceived greatness. This of course misaligns Mozart further, causing his difficulties to worsen. As both Fatal Flaws develop into mad obsessions, a vicious cycle of action and counter-action develops between Salieri and Mozart. Salieri's acts of jealousy motivate Mozart to escalate his acts of pride, which in turn inflame Salieri's jealousy further. This eventually builds to a crisis event in which it becomes clear that these two prideful egos cannot continue to coexist. One must be eliminated.

If Salieri were a better man, he would take this crisis as proof that he was beaten, accept Mozart as the more talented, and extend grace unto him. Instead, Salieri chooses to put the Nail in his Coffin. Salieri concludes that the only remaining option is to cause Mozart's death. With this, Salieri crosses the point of no return. Until now, all his actions may have been forgiven. But this is an intentional act of evil that condemns Salieri to his eventual damnation. Yet this plan only succeeds due to Mozart's own obsession with this Fatal Flaw. When Salieri approaches Mozart in the guise of Mozart's dead father, Mozart is compelled to accept Salieri's offer out of a desire to prove his greatness to the cold, graceless father who challenged his pride in life. With this, Mozart puts the Nail in his own Coffin as well. He falls into Salieri's trap and works himself to death because his pride will not allow him otherwise. This begins the downward spiral of the third act which leads both characters to ruin.

Though Salieri technically achieves his goal by killing Mozart, he does not receive any reward. Reward comes only to those who accept the controlling value. Instead, the story world punishes Salieri with madness. With added irony, Salieri must watch as the fame he defended with such jealousy fades away while his rival's work lives on. Salieri ends up pathetic and alone, with nothing left to be proud of, all because he could not find the grace or humility to accept someone greater than he.

## *Citizen Kane*

When analyzed, the psychology of *Citizen Kane* turns out to be extremely Freudian. The protagonist Charles Foster Kane is a victim of arrested development. Though he is brilliant, ambitious, and charismatic, Kane is an underdeveloped man-child in terms of his emotional maturity. Kane was taken from his mother at a young age and raised to adulthood by cold-hearted millionaire Walter Thatcher. This seems to have been extremely traumatic for Kane, for when he reaches adulthood, Kane is driven to use all his wealth and charm to regain the childhood love he was once denied. This is Kane's Story Goal: to somehow, some way achieve a position in which he will receive the love of the whole world.

However, Kane does not want just any love. He expects the kind of love only a mother can give; one eternal and unconditional that requires nothing in return. Yet this is misguided. When a child grows, he or she eventually learns that love is a two-way street. One must give love in order to receive it. But Kane has never reached this understanding. His mind remains trapped in an immature paradigm, continuing to expect a mother's love from everyone and everything. Whenever Kane finds that love has conditions attached, he misconstrues it as a personal rejection. Rather than learn and grow from the experience, Kane becomes angry and disappointed, leading to increasingly childish behaviors that worsen his situation.

This might seem tragic if it were not for the methods Kane uses to pursue this love. Whether it be as a newspaper man, a politician, or a friend and husband, Kane manipulates people in ways that border on the sociopathic. Though Kane initially apes the story world's controlling value of reciprocal love by pretending to be a magnanimous individual, his behavior is in fact deeply misaligned. He gives no love to others and wants it only for himself. While Kane finds some early success through these tactics, the story world eventually cracks down on Kane with a series of failures that end in total defeat.

In the first act, Kane pursues the love of the world with great zeal, establishing himself as a so-called champion of the people by mercilessly attacking his former father figure Walter Thatcher. (It is hard to deny the Freudian psychology of *Kane* as we see the protagonist attack his father to seek the love of a mother in a classic Oedipal complex.) Soon Kane becomes the most successful newsman in New York. However, the love of Kane's readers and staff are not enough for him. Like a child, he demands more.

Kane marries Emily Norton, the niece of the President. This marriage is not out of love. He is only "collecting" her, the same way he collected his newspaper staff. Emily is just a rung on a ladder Kane hopes to climb to achieve his eventual goal. Yet this marriage does not turn out as Kane planned. Because Kane's Flaw prevents him from returning Emily's love, the marriage grows cold. Rather than realize this mistake and make an effort to save his marriage, Kane seeks affection elsewhere in a new lover, Susan Alexander. Yet the private love of two women is still not enough for Kane. He wants the love of the entire public and nearly gets it with a whirlwind campaign for governor. (To do this, Kane simply transfers the target of his Oedipal complex from Thatcher to the incumbent governor Jim Geddes.)

True to narrative form, Kane's flawed ways catch up to him at the story's Midpoint. Kane's extramarital affair is discovered by Jim Geddes and used for blackmail. Here, Kane faces his Crucial Decision. A man of emotional maturity would take this as a cue to reevaluate himself, admit his mistakes, and bow out of the election with dignity. This would give Kane an opportunity to reform his life and pursue happiness through more reasonable means. Instead, Kane throws a tantrum. Blinded by his Flaw, he rejects Geddes' deal, saying he will not let anyone "take the love of the voters" away from him, as if he genuinely expects the world to love him unconditionally. This of course turns out to be untrue. By refusing to change, Kane destroys his marriage along with his political career.

While some might take this defeat as a lesson, Kane takes it personally. The people revoked their love for him in the same way his mother once did. In response, Kane intensifies his flawed behavior. He tries to bully the world into loving him again by using poor Susan Alexander as his pawn. Since these actions are even more misaligned than the previous, they fail even worse. Kane becomes a laughingstock, loses his friends, and drives Susan to attempt suicide.

Yet Kane continues to refuse any lesson. His Flaw has grown into an obsession and can only see this as another rejection. Kane matches this childish evaluation with an equally childish response. Kane puts the Nail in his Coffin by isolating himself in his fortress Xanadu, essentially rejecting the world he believes rejected him. Kane takes only Susan with him, but even in this two-person universe, Kane cannot learn to give love in order to get it back. Susan is not willing to put up the cold, flaw-obsessed man Kane has become and leaves him. Still, Kane refuses to learn anything. His only response is to throw his most childish tantrum yet.

Kane ends up dying bitter and alone, a little boy still trapped in an old man's body, all because he failed to recognize his Flaw and realign himself with the values controlling his world. One little flaw ruined what could have been a great man, providing a Cautionary lesson that while lost on Kane is hopefully not lost on the audience.

# THE TRAGIC

In the Tragic narrative, the protagonist possesses, embodies, or champions a quality the viewing audience considers admirable. However, the character exists in a story world that refuses to support this quality and instead rewards the opposite. This means the supposed virtue is actually a flaw. Clinging to this flawed virtue dooms the protagonist to failure no matter how hard he or she fights or how noble his or her intentions. The purpose of the Tragic narrative is to show how certain socially-glorified values or beliefs can prove false, inadequate, or even destructive within certain contexts. The audience is then led to reevaluate the value or belief, or question society's failure to support it.

## *Chinatown*

Jake Gittes is a private investigator. As such, he exists in the murky gray area between crime and the law. In such a morally-ambiguous environment, a good private investigator must rely on more than his gun or his intuition. He needs a sense of integrity. Without the will to abide by a strong set of ethical convictions, a private eye can easily forget about right or wrong, and succumb to the corruption around him.

Jake Gittes may not be a man of the highest moral fiber, but he is a man who greatly values his professional integrity. He is the best at what he does and will not allow anyone to cast disparagement upon it. It is for this reason that Gittes becomes so upset when he learns a phony client has played him for a sap. When Hollis Mulwray winds up dead, possibly as a result of Gittes' involvement, Gittes is driven to get to the bottom of the mystery, not so much out of a sense of justice, but to restore integrity to his name.

Yet something separates *Chinatown* from more traditional stories in the detective vein. Most films in the genre are Celebratory in nature, ultimately rewarding the hero's personal ethics and punishing the immoral or corrupt. *Chinatown* does not end this way. In a reversal of expectations, Gittes fails in the end. Despite relentlessly following his sense of integrity, despite fighting and sacrificing for what he believes to be right, Gittes receives nothing but punishment in the end. This is because Gittes' story world does not reward the value of integrity. It rewards the opposite: Corruption.

*Chinatown*'s Los Angeles is irreconcilably corrupt. It is filled with lies, scandal, and conspiracy. This is not a temporary aberration from the story world's true nature like in *The Shawshank Redemption*. This *is* the world's true nature. Corruption is the controlling value. The more corrupt the individual, the more he or she profits. Men of integrity end up punished. This story world does not see Gittes as a hero, but as a troublemaker. Like Jake La Motta, Antonio Salieri, and Charles Foster Kane, Jake Gittes embraces a value his world soundly rejects. This means there is no way for Gittes' story to end in anything but failure.

Gittes however is ignorant of his misalignment. He mistakenly believes championing the value of integrity will allow him to come out on top. This is a false paradigm, and therefore Gittes' Fatal Flaw. Gittes' integrity brings him nothing but trouble as the story unfolds. It is out of integrity that Gittes sticks his nose in the situation rather than let sleeping dogs lie. It is out of integrity that Gittes chooses to dig himself in deeper when harassed by thugs, tempted by money, and begged off with promises and lies. Each encounter should convince Gittes to abandon his course of action. Yet each time, Gittes ignores these warnings and charges further down a road that can only lead to his defeat. This is what makes *Chinatown* tragic. Gittes rarely commits an action the audience does not support. Yet still, he is punished due to the unjust rules of his corrupt story world.

As always, Gittes' actions lead him to a moment of Crucial Decision at the story's Midpoint. Noah Cross, the story's antagonist and chief force of corruption, offers to pay Gittes double if he drops his investigation and agrees to work for him. Cross essentially asks Gittes to convert to the side of corruption. If Gittes accepts this offer, he might eventually profit from the situation. Instead, Gittes turns Cross down. With this, Gittes makes it clear that he will align himself against the controlling value and continue to fight against the story world.

Just like Jake La Motta or Antonio Salieri, Gittes becomes obsessed with his Flaw in Act 2B. What was once a mere sense of professional integrity transforms into a far more potent moral integrity. This compels Gittes to take actions he never would have before. Unfortunately, this misaligns Gittes further, causing him to entrench himself into an increasingly threatening situation. This inevitably leads to a crisis event. Gittes has found evidence that suggests Mrs. Mulwray is her husband's killer. Despite the romance between her and Gittes, pressure from the LAPD demands he bring her in. Yet when Gittes tries to arrest Mrs. Mulwray, he discovers the dark secret at the heart of the mystery. Confronted by the shocking truth of just how corrupt his story world really is, Gittes faces a dilemma. If Gittes does what he is told, he will save his skin, but play right into Noah Cross's hands. If he follows his moral integrity and helps Mrs. Mulwray, he will do what is right but risk everything he has. Gittes chooses the latter. Though this seems valiant to the audience, this puts the Nail in Gittes' Coffin. By rejecting his last opportunity to conform to the controlling value, Gittes inadvertently initiates a downward spiral of events that ends up helping Cross, harming Mrs. Mulwray, and leading Gittes to defeat. Thus, by clinging to his Flaw, Gittes creates an end far worse than what would have happened if he had done nothing at all.

The natural alignment of the story world reasserts itself in the final resolution. The story world always wins, whether it be by nature good or evil. So, the forces of corruption are rewarded while integrity is defeated. This reversal of audience expectations presents a more complex message than that found in a Celebratory or Cautionary tale. Rather than blindly glorify a social ideal, *Chinatown* shows how society often fails to reward a value it supposedly supports. While society promotes integrity in principle, it too often allows the corrupt to succeed. Through its Tragic end, *Chinatown* proves the world is not always the good and just place we believe it to be.

## *Braveheart*

The duality between opposing values in a Tragic narrative need not always be as morally black-or-white as they are in *Chinatown*. Sometimes, the world-supported value is neither inherently good nor evil, but may lead to both depending upon its use. When used prudently, the value may lead to the greater good. When abused, for instance at the hands of the antagonist, it can cause much wrong. However, the protagonist may see only the abuses and assume the value to be a bad thing. This creates a flawed paradigm that aligns the protagonist against the controlling value, causing him or her to fight against what he or she is better off embracing. This ignorance dooms the protagonist to fail, no matter how brave, noble, or virtuous his or her intentions may be.

William Wallace, the protagonist of *Braveheart,* can be described by many terms. He is courageous, honorable, pure of heart, and affectionate of spirit. Most importantly, he is uncompromising. In many contexts, the word "uncompromising" is considered a distinction of greatness. Civil servants are praised for uncompromising dedication. Companies pride themselves on uncompromising service. Great filmmakers are idolized for uncompromising visions. At its most positive, the word implies an unyielding dedication to an extremely high set of personal standards. In this way, we consider William Wallace's uncompromising nature admirable. He fights for the absolute freedom of his countrymen and will accept no lesser outcome. However, there is a downside to this nature. A refusal to compromise can make one pig-headed or uncooperative. It can lead one to reject sensible solutions in favor of impractical ideals. An uncompromising nature often blinds a person to the pragmatic nature of reality and the less-than-perfect outcomes he or she must often accept to survive.

In this way, Wallace's uncompromising nature is both his greatest virtue and his deepest flaw. For though Wallace behaves like a valiant knight, 13th century Scotland is not the simple land of a fairy tale. Despite its rustic appearance, it is a land ruled by politics. The Scottish state stands fractured amongst rival clans and nobles, all living in subservience to a tyrant English king. Since each noble must contend with his contemporaries as well as the overwhelming power of the English, these men must seek sensible ways to preserve their interests through compromise and cooperation. This turns compromise into the story's controlling value. However, political compromise allows only a slow and unsatisfying rate of progress. Furthermore, the English king Edward Longshanks has abused this practice at the expense of the Scots many times in the past. This causes Wallace to misinterpret compromise as weak, cowardly, and ineffective. Wallace rejects compromise in any form and chooses to pursue his goals through direct and open insurrection. Though this simple-minded idealism allows Wallace some surprise victories in the story's first half, this flaw disguised as a virtue ultimately becomes the tool by which Wallace digs his own grave.

Wallace's bold, uncompromising actions motivate Longshanks to send a full army north to crush the Scots in battle. The Scottish nobles know they are outmatched, so as customary plan to negotiate a compromise so they might gain something without bloodshed. Yet Wallace will not stand for this. In his moment of Crucial Decision, Wallace sabotages negotiations so that battle will ensue. Though some brilliant tactics allow a surprise victory, Wallace's rejection of the controlling value complicates matters and worsens his situation. Since it is clear Wallace will not compromise, Longshanks sees no option but to kill Wallace. Meanwhile, the Scottish nobles are led to believe Wallace is a dangerous and uncontrollable individual whom they cannot support. Following their nature of compromise, the nobles negotiate a deal to betray Wallace in battle. Because of Wallace's refusal to align with the controlling value, his army is handed a terrible defeat, creating the story's crisis event.

Yet as typical in Tragic narratives, Wallace refuses to learn from this defeat. Instead of doing the sensible thing and reconciling with the nobles, Wallace puts the Nail in his Coffin by launching a campaign of bloody revenge. By allowing his Flaw to grow into an obsession, Wallace becomes an enemy to both sides. This provokes the nobles to betray Wallace once more, this time directly into the hands of the English—once again proving that those who compromise win out over those who do not.

Yet even when helpless, imprisoned, and doomed to execution, Wallace refuses to abandon his Fatal Flaw. He spits out the elixir given to numb his pain and endures unimaginable agony by refusing to ask for mercy. Even in his last moments, Wallace remains so uncompromising that he will not utter a single word to end his suffering. Though our hearts go out to Wallace, though it is impossible not to admire such strength of character, this final refusal accomplishes nothing. Wallace still dies. He dies tragically because of his failure to yield his nature to a simple value that may have provided a far better end.

By showing how an admired quality may lead to ruin, a story such as *Braveheart* warns an audience that blind or incautious excesses of virtue can become a double-edged sword. Social values must be applied prudently and intelligently. Otherwise, a virtue becomes a vice and negative consequences will ensue.

## One Flew Over the Cuckoo's Nest

*One Flew Over the Cuckoo's Nest* takes place inside a mental hospital. Mental hospitals are by nature institutions of conformity. Patients are there due to the extreme nonconformity of their behavior and are "cured" when they have reformed their thoughts and actions to social norms. The world of Cuckoo's Nest enforces conformity. This is its controlling value.

Though sometimes spoken of disparagingly, conformity is not necessarily a bad thing. Society could not function without it. As seen frequently in *Cuckoo's Nest*, it is impossible to have so much as a game of cards or a simple conversation if individuals do not abide by certain norms of behavior. Conformity causes harm only when it restricts personal freedoms. To prevent this from happening, our society matches conformity with a counter-value: Individualism. By supporting two opposing values at once, society achieves a sense of balance. One value counter-acts the other, ensuring that neither is taken to excess. However, harmful complications will ensue if this relationship becomes imbalanced. *One Flew Over the Cuckoo's Nest* uses its narrative to examine the excesses of both conformity and individualism in an effort to find where their balance should lie.

Protagonist R.P. McMurphy might be considered the ultimate individualist. He does not like anyone telling him how to think or behave. Though we admire McMurphy for his spirit, his sense of self-determination, and the enthusiasm with which he chases the pleasures of life, McMurphy often takes these qualities to harmful extremes. McMurphy's faulty mental paradigm causes him to misinterpret any force of conformity as a personal threat, even when its presence is benign or beneficial. He then rebels in situations that do not call for it, creating trouble for himself and others. By inserting the ultimate individualist into the ultimate world of conformity, *Cuckoo's Nest* quickly establishes both its Thematic Argument and its dramatic conflict. In no time at all, McMurphy comes into conflict with Nurse Ratched, the chief force of conformity in this world. With an irresistible force meeting an immovable object, something must eventually give. But which will it be, the individualism or the conformity?

McMurphy makes this conflict official at the end of Act 1 when he wagers he can steal control of the ward away from Nurse Ratched. However, this turns out to be no easy task. McMurphy's attitude of extreme individualism is deeply misaligned with his story world and his attempts to move against the grain meet nothing but resistance. This leads to a Crucial Decision at the story's Midpoint. McMurphy can either make his life easier by cooperating with Ratched and the hospital, or he can follow his Flaw and stage an open revolt. McMurphy chooses revolt by climbing the fence to take his fellow patients on an unsanctioned field trip. By deliberately choosing to remain misaligned, McMurphy meets swift consequences. The hospital decides it will no longer release McMurphy after thirty days, but keep him there indefinitely.

Rather than learn a lesson from this, McMurphy clings tighter to his Flaw and ups the ante, leading to a violent revolt in the day room. This aggressive counter-attack by the force of individualism demands an equal response from the forces of conformity. The hospital punishes McMurphy with shock therapy. But this once again does nothing to convince McMurphy to change. Rather than give in to conformity, McMurphy takes his misalignment to its extreme with a plan that ends up putting the Nail in his Coffin. Simply escaping the hospital is not enough for McMurphy. He has to indulge his Fatal Flaw to its fullest by throwing a raucous party before leaving just to snub his nose at Nurse Ratched on his way out.

Yet of course, this all goes awry. When Nurse Ratched discovers what McMurphy has done, she cracks down with such fury that it drives one of McMurphy's comrades to suicide. Seeing conformity at its worst causes

McMurphy to snap. He shows his own Flaw at its ugliest by strangling Nurse Ratched. Of course, McMurphy's escalation must be met once more. McMurphy's continued refusal to accept the controlling value leaves the story world no other option than to reassert its control by destroying McMurphy completely. McMurphy is lobotomized, permanently taking away his sense of individualism and defeating him once and for all.

Though McMurphy fails tragically, *One Flew Over the Cuckoo's Nest* does not conclude as dispiritingly as this suggests. Unlike *Chinatown,* where one thematic element is clearly right and the other wrong, the Thematic Argument of *Cuckoo's Nest* regards the *balance* between two equally necessary values. As such, we find that McMurphy's actions have not been a total failure. His presence has instilled life and spirit back into those locked inside the hospital's walls. Because of this, the film ends not in despair, but with a sense of hope as we watch Chief escape the hospital to reclaim his own individualism. Here we see the further nuance the Tragic narrative is capable of communicating as opposed to the Celebratory or Cautionary. *Cuckoo's Nest* condemns neither individualism nor conformity. It only condemns their excesses. With an end that is a failure in once sense but a victory in another, *Cuckoo's Nest* provides both a celebration and a warning. It states that society needs both values, but in a healthy and harmonious balance.

# THE CYNICAL

The Cynical narrative combines the structure of the Celebratory with the social criticism of the Tragic to deliver a darker and far more unsettling message. The Cynical takes the Celebratory through the looking-glass into a world where everything is reversed. Black is white. Light is dark. Right is wrong. The protagonist begins the story hampered by beliefs we have been taught to consider good, healthy, or true. However, events cause the protagonist to realize these beliefs are myths, delusions, or outright lies. If the protagonist is to survive, he or she must abandon society's misleading beliefs and realign with the true values of his or her world, as objectionable or horrifying as they may be. By presenting an outcome opposed to what society teaches, Cynical narratives directly challenge the audience's beliefs. Though they may be harsh, cold, and unsettling, Cynical narratives serve a vital function by forcing audiences to look through society's illusions to the darker truths on the other side.

## *The Godfather*

"It's not personal. It's just business." Organized crime is a harsh trade. A family like the Corleones must commit daily acts of immorality just to survive. This is not because the Corleones are evil. It is simply a requirement of their world. Murder is a necessary evil in the world of *The Godfather*. There is no real hatred. It is just a part of doing business.

To understand this world and the slow, cumulative effect it can have on an individual, it must be observed through the eyes of an outsider with whom the audience can identify. Protagonist Michael Corleone has been intentionally kept out of the family business. He has gone to college and served in the military, giving him an idealist sense of morality that is far more in line with mainstream American society than his family's old Sicilian ways. "That's my family," he tells Kay, "That's not me." The conflict between Michael's beliefs and those of his world establishes a Thematic Argument of *moral idealism* versus *moral practicality*. Moral practicality is not the same as immorality. It means one continues to hold a moral code, but one flexible enough to bend, break, or ignore the laws of God and man when justified by the situation. The high-minded ideals Michael acquired in college and the military are great in theory, but they are not practical in the world of organized crime. Therefore, Michael's idealistic beliefs constitute his Fatal Flaw. *The Godfather* uses the Cynical narrative to portray the re-education of Michael Corleone. The plot provides a chain of events that force Michael to reevaluate his beliefs and realign them with the practical morality of his world.

Michael's re-education begins when his father Vito is gunned down for refusing a deal with the gangster Virgil Sollozzo. With Vito clinging to life in the hospital, the idealist Michael believes Sollozzo will play by the rules and not try to kill a helpless man. However, Michael discovers he is wrong. Trapped for the first time in the type of life-or-death situation all too common in the mafia world, Michael must momentarily think like a gangster to save his father's life. Rebuffed by this, Sollozzo requests a meeting with Michael, thinking that Michael's moral idealism will make him weak. However, the incident at the hospital has shown Michael that Sollozzo will stop at nothing to harm his family. In this situation, the only morally practical act is to kill Sollozzo. With little other choice, Michael decides he must temporarily put aside his moral idealism. He will kill Sollozzo himself.

Though Michael does kill Sollozzo, this action does not yet convert him to the dark side. This is meant to be a one-time act, a single indiscretion from his accustomed ways. When Michael is sent to Sicily to wait out the situation, he falls back into the life of a civilian. He marries a local girl, believing he can still have a morally-idealistic existence separate from the family business. But once more, reality proves Michael wrong. He learns his brother Sonny has been killed and then watches his new wife die in an attempt on his own life. With this, Michael finally realizes that moral ideals mean nothing in this world. Morals are worthless if no one chooses to obey them. Michael now understands that unless he wants to see more loved ones die, he too must abandon all moral ideals. With this, Michael converts. He will now act with moral practicality rather than any of his former beliefs.

Upon returning home, Michael's change in character is astonishing. He has become cold, calculating, and more than willing to step into the shoes of his father. But just like any Celebratory protagonist, Michael struggles with this transition. Friend and foe alike have difficulty taking Michael seriously. Michael's conversion has yet to be tested. This test arrives with the crisis event at the beginning of the third act. Vito Corleone has died. With the patriarch gone, the family's enemies will strike at Michael's fledgling leadership in an attempt to destroy the Corleones once and for all. How will Michael respond? With the cold, remorseless practicality necessary to survive? Or will Michael fall back on his Flaw and let moral idealism make him weak?

Michael's answer is strong and unequivocal. While the old Michael would never attack first, the new Michael completes his conversion by launching a bloody campaign of surprise attacks that eliminate all his enemies in one fell swoop. There is no moral idealism left in Michael. He simply does what must be done. Michael has fully realigned himself with moral practicality—not because he wanted to, but because the situation demanded it—and in the process abandoned the part of himself society considers "good." This point is driven home through the eyes of the story's one remaining outsider Kay. She recognizes that Michael is no longer the man she once loved. To survive, Michael has thrown away his soul.

*The Godfather* is unique among our study films in that its epic scope and sprawling narrative require its lead role to shift away from Michael to Vito or Sonny in certain sequences in an ensemble fashion. However, the narrative remains cohesive by the fact that the dilemma between moral idealism and moral practicality continues in these characters as well. The attempt on Vito's life comes after Vito allows his morals to influence his business decisions. Eventually, Vito abandons his moral objections to ensure his family's safety. Sonny struggles with this dilemma in a much different way. Sonny does not think pragmatically. His moral ideals compel him towards wrath and vengeance. This puts him into conflict with Tom Hagen. Tom also struggles with this dilemma, arguing for peace and reconciliation even when bloodshed is absolutely necessary. Despite its many threads, *The*

*Godfather* remains a unified drama with every element addressing the same question from different angles. Together, the film delivers a single message: Moral ideals are not practical. Survival must be treated like a business; one that requires cold, practical decisions where moral ideals can hold no part.

## The Silence of the Lambs

It is no accident that *The Silence of the Lambs* opens with its protagonist running through the forest, looking tired, lost, and desperate. This is the first of many allusions to Little Red Riding Hood, the tale of a girl who grows older and wiser after encountering a beast in the deep, dark woods. In the world of *The Silence of the Lambs*, monsters really do lurk in the darkness; real-life monsters ready to prey upon any innocent who should pass by. To survive, one must come to understand this darkness, accept this darkness, and find the will to gaze into it without weakness or fear.

Like *The Godfather*, *The Silence of the Lambs* portrays the re-education of its young protagonist into the true workings of her world. To do this, *Lambs* takes an interesting twist on the traditional mentor-and-apprentice relationship seen in many other films. Hannibal Lecter is not the story's villain. He is Clarice Starling's Obi-Wan Kenobi, her Morpheus, her Gandalf the Grey. Yet unlike these mentors, Lecter does not elevate Starling by imparting righteous ideals. He instead leads her deep down into the darkness to reveal the truths most people would rather deny. Starling's Story Goal is to catch serial killer Buffalo Bill. To do so, she must learn to think like Bill. Rather than fear Bill's darkness, she must understand it. For as Lecter knows, this story world rewards those who accept the darkness, not those who hide from it.

This Thematic Argument is given further substance by the fact that Starling has not one but two potential mentors, both vying to pull her in their own direction. Opposite Hannibal Lecter is the FBI's Jack Crawford. Unlike Lecter, Crawford is a man of procedure. He approaches the problem of Buffalo Bill with the cold detachment of a bureaucrat; through charts and graphs, computers and psychological profiles. Thanks to her training at the FBI Academy, Starling begins her story under the same mindset.

However, in this story world, this mindset is a Fatal Flaw. Those who trust procedure really do so out of fear. They believe that by hiding behind an impersonal wall of regulations they can protect themselves from the evil they face. Yet as the narrative unfolds, we find that those who put their faith in procedure always fail. Crawford fails. Senator Ruth Martin fails. The guards at the Tennessee courthouse fail. Lecter proves them all fools because Lecter is aligned with the nature of his story world while they are not.

The course of Starling's transformation (and in connection the course of the plot) unfolds largely through a series of encounters between Starling and Hannibal Lecter in which Lecter slowly leads Starling away from the FBI's flawed perspective toward one closer aligned with her story world. After each encounter, Starling uses what Lecter has imparted to take one step closer to finding Buffalo Bill. However, it should be noted that Lecter knows Bill's identity from the start. He could simply tell Starling how to catch Bill, but this would defeat the purpose of a mentor. A mentor's role is to shape the apprentice in such a way that the apprentice becomes capable of accomplishing the ultimate task all by him or herself. Therefore, Hannibal Lecter functions as the story's catalyst for character change.

However, this change is extremely difficult for Starling. Lecter is a harsh and frightening mentor. He answers Starling's questions with riddles and in return demands Starling reveal traumatic secrets from her past. He does this not out of some perverse pleasure, but because he knows it to be essential for Starling's transformation. To catch Bill, Starling must understand Bill's dark compulsions, and the best way to do this is for Starling to recognize similar compulsions in herself. Yet due to her Flaw, Starling initially fears this darkness and continually falls back on Crawford's ineffective methods. Whenever this occurs, Lecter pushes Starling away with a puzzle to solve. Starling must venture out into the darkness and return only when she has learned what Lecter is trying to impart.

Starling's resistance to Lecter ends at the story's Midpoint. Until this moment, Starling has only met with Lecter because she was ordered by the FBI. Yet now she comes to Lecter without permission and by her own free will. With this, Starling makes her Crucial Decision. She has concluded that

Lecter's ways are far more powerful than Crawford's and becomes willing to surrender to Lecter's darkness to achieve her Story Goal. Here, Starling passes the final step of her apprenticeship by confessing the childhood incident at the heart of her compulsion to find Bill. Lecter thanks her afterward, again not out of some sick pleasure, but as a reward. By admitting her darkest compulsion and revealing the demon inside her, Starling shows she is now willing to openly face the darkness and embraces the story world's controlling value.

With this accomplished, Lecter disappears, leaving Starling to solve the rest of the mystery on her own. Like all stories built upon mentorship such as *Star Wars, The Matrix,* or *The Lord of the Rings: The Fellowship of the Ring,* the mentor must leave at some point to force the apprentice to stand on his or her own two feet. Due to her new willingness to journey into the darkness rather than hide from it, Starling finds success, discovering clues that Crawford could never see. Yet like Michael in *The Godfather,* her final test has yet to come. So far, Starling has only experienced the world's evil from a safe and controlled distance. To complete her training, Little Red Riding Hood must enter the Wolf's den and meet the Beast eye-to-eye.

A twist of fate imposes the story's crisis event. Starling is shocked to find herself face to face with Buffalo Bill with nothing to protect her. Starling could run away or make the fatal mistake of falling back on procedure, but doing so would allow Bill to escape. Instead, Starling fully embraces the controlling value by following the monster into its lair. While the old Starling would have perished in this situation, the transformed Starling succeeds. She finds her way through the darkness (literally) and kills the monster. This victory would have been impossible had Lecter not taught Starling to abandon Crawford's flawed methods and look evil unflinchingly in the eye.

Since *The Silence of the Lambs* ends with Bill defeated, one might misconstrue the film to be Celebratory in nature and attribute Starling's success to another, more socially-uplifting quality. Yet if this story world were in fact good and pure, Hannibal Lecter would not have been allowed to remain free at the story's end. No, this is indeed a world of darkness, and by contributing to Lecter's escape, Starling has reverted the Cynical world back to its natural order. At first glance, Starling's defeat of Bill (good triumphing over evil) and Lecter's permanent escape (evil triumphing over good) seems to provide a contradictory resolution. Yet it is with this supposed contradiction that *The Silence of the Lambs* puts the exclamation point upon its intended message. *Lambs* rejects the prevailing social notion that good and evil can be kept separate. In its natural state, good and evil will always intermingle, both in society and in ourselves. We all have dark compulsions. Some indulge these compulsions, some resist them. But like Starling, we cannot hide from them. The only way to control the balance between good and evil is to understand these dark compulsions, in others as well as in ourselves. For no good comes from hiding from the truth.

## *Apocalypse Now*

War is a state of madness. It is chaos. It is savagery. It is an indefinitely prolonged nightmare for anyone involved. In a world where all has succumbed to madness, the only true insanity comes from those who cling to delusions of normalcy or control. This is the primary substance of *Apocalypse Now*. Its story world is aligned with madness. It supports and rewards those who embrace this madness and gives no aid to those who try to impose the absurd illusions of a civilized world.

Captain Benjamin Willard is ordered into the depths of the Cambodian jungle by high-ranking American officers to find and kill Colonel Walter E. Kurtz, a man whom Willard is told has gone dangerously insane. However, as the film illustrates, Kurtz's mental state is a matter of perspective. To Kurtz, it is the commanding officers who are insane. These men live a contradiction. They order atrocities. They are personally responsible for the deaths of thousands, yet continue to behave as if they were civilized gentlemen. All Kurtz has done is correct the contradiction. He openly admits that he is a savage and makes no excuses for the sickening acts he commits in the name of war. His experiences have taught him the true nature of his story world, provoking him to realign with its controlling value.

The narrative of *Apocalypse Now* portrays the same transformation in Willard. Willard seems partially aware of his world's madness as the story begins, yet he fights against this by continuing to think and behave in the way the outside world expects. The Army has taught Willard to look upon chaos and madness and pretend it to be order and sanity. This mindset constitutes Willard's Fatal Flaw. As long as Willard continues to think in the way the military has taught, he will remain unable to accept this world for what it is and adopt the behaviors necessary to survive.

As the narrative unfolds, progressively-escalating incidents of chaos and absurdity slowly wear away at Willard's false paradigm. Any attempt to impose a sense of normalcy or control inevitably devolves into madness. Eventually, Willard can no longer deny the true nature of his world, prompting him to correct the contradictions in his behavior just as Kurtz once did. Willard makes his Crucial Decision at the story's Midpoint by shooting an injured woman rather than follow military regulations. Willard rightfully recognizes the Army's rules to be absurd and pointless. They do nothing but enforce false delusions of order and civility. With this action, Willard makes the conscious choice to pursue the rest of his mission according to Kurtz's rules, not those taught by the military.

If Willard has any lingering faith in order or sanity, it is progressively stripped away in the story's second half. The further Willard continues downriver, the more psychotic the world becomes. Willard faces his crisis event upon entering the heart of all madness, Colonel Kurtz's compound. Captured and utterly helpless, Willard has no choice but to abandon any last notion of sanity and surrender himself to Colonel Kurtz's tutelage, for to do otherwise would bring certain death. With this, Kurtz completes Willard's re-education and Willard fully embraces the madness.

Though Willard eventually fulfills his mission by killing Kurtz, he does not do so because he was ordered by the military. He kills Kurtz because the story world commands him to do it. As Willard puts it, "Even the jungle wanted him dead. And that's who he took his orders from anyway." Willard has reached full conversion. He is no longer a soldier, but a servant of the controlling value. In the end, all illusions of sanity have disappeared and all succumbs to madness, reverting the story world back to its natural order.

\* \* \*

"You must make a friend of horror. Horror and mortal terror are your friends. If they are not, they are enemies to be feared." This line spoken by Kurtz summarizes the philosophy of the Cynical narrative. To survive, protagonists must ignore socially-constructed notions of ethics and morality, for as Kurtz says, "It is judgment that defeats us." Michael Corleone, Clarice Starling, and Captain Willard are all at first blinded by the inaccurate beliefs and false systems of judgment imposed by outside society, but eventually open their eyes to the true natures of their worlds. Since these true natures are often dark and unsettling, Cynical narratives imply that what we have been taught to believe as "right" or "true" might actually be a lie. The Cynical narrative uses the ugliest of lessons to draw attention to the harmful aspects of society or human nature that continue to exist despite the systems of belief we have constructed to the contrary.

In conclusion, the Celebratory and Cautionary narratives provide lessons on how the world "should" be. They present models of behavior or systems of ethics we are expected to emulate, both as individuals and as a society as a whole. The Tragic and Cynical narratives are created to remind us of the less than satisfactory state our world continues to exist within; due either to a failure to properly implement our values or some flaw in the beliefs attached to those values. Instead of looking forward towards some ideal, the Tragic and Cynical urge us to look backwards at our mistakes so we may hopefully fix what we have broken. In either case, the story communicates its message in the same way. The protagonist is presented with a choice of values and is then rewarded or punished because of that choice. The audience compares this outcome to their current beliefs and renders an ideological conclusion. This is the process of cinematic storytelling. One structure, four thematic types, an infinite number of possibilities.

## CHAPTER 1-7
# COMPLICATING ISSUES

As with any "universal" model, the unified narrative structure contains instances of deviation, variation, and exception from the norm, both major and minor. These instances are natural and inevitable. Every dramatic structure requires flexibility. As said before, structure must adjust to meet the needs of the story, not the other way around. Specific elements of a story's premise or ideological message may require the narrative to break from standard form. However, when deviation occurs, it is important to consider whether the storyteller chose to intentionally disregard structural rules to benefit the narrative, or if deviation simply occurred due to a lack of skill or foresight, ultimately harming the story's potential.

As such, deviation may help or hinder a narrative. Deviation is acceptable, even laudable if done for a purpose that better serves the story or its audience. However, the storyteller must know with certainty what he or she is doing and why. Dramatists use the word "structure" in conscious allusion to the field of engineering. A structure is an arrangement of elements organized in such a way to maintain the physical integrity of an overall design. If one removes or changes a piece of that structure, the alteration must be compensated elsewhere; otherwise the entire design may collapse. In the same way, deviation in screencraft should not occur randomly and without reason. With every alteration, the storyteller should realize what is lost and take pains to compensate in other areas or else it will be the narrative that collapses, losing the audience with it.

But why is deviation sometimes necessary to tell an effective story? The answer is closely related to certain criticisms sure to arise from a narrow-minded evaluation of the unified narrative structure. First, some may claim that dividing all cinematic narratives into four thematic types (Celebratory, Cautionary, Tragic, and Cynical) oversimplifies storytelling and does not allow for stories that may intentionally avoid absolute character transformation or clear-cut dramatic resolutions. Others may object to the unified structure's emphasis on thematic duality. By regarding the conflict between theme and anti-theme as the locus of all narrative content, the unified narrative structure favors a diametric approach where every significant element must be arranged on one side of the thematic divide or the other. Some may feel this limits storytelling only to narratives with clear, authoritarian lessons, preventing the possibility of open-ended discourse for issues where solutions may be unclear. Both criticisms allude to the same thing. Any truly universal structure must allow room for cases of *ambiguity*.

In most areas of storytelling, ambiguity is a bad thing. Ambiguity within plot means actions or events are confusing or unclear, making the story difficult to follow. Ambiguity within character means motivations are vague or nonexistent, making it difficult to assign meaning to actions or empathize with behaviors. The only area of screencraft in which ambiguity may be desirable is in the outcome of the Thematic Argument. This is not to say a storyteller should ever be uncertain about what message he or she intends to impart. This means it is sometimes desirable to resolve the Character Arc or Story Spine in a way that leaves the Thematic Argument open to debate after the story has ended. Not all questions have easy answers. Many stories address personal or social dilemmas that have no immediate solution. In these cases, it may be preferable, or even required, to resolve the story with a deliberate lack of full thematic closure so the audience is left with a feeling of irresolution, hopefully encouraging further reflection upon the story's events. While a story without thematic ambiguity gives a strong and direct message, stories with ambiguous resolutions can stay with audiences longer as they search for greater meanings which may lay outside the story's physical content.

## CAUSES OF AMBIGUITY

As established by the Thematic Matrix, a cinematic story's ultimate message is primarily dependent upon two factors: *a)* the value chosen by the protagonist at the Crucial Decision (specifically whether this is a socially-approved value or a socially-disapproved value), and *b)* whether this value leads the protagonist to success or failure. Generally, thematic ambiguity is created by injecting some form of uncertainty into one or both of these areas. Though not an exclusive list, here follows a selection of ways this may be accomplished.

### *Value Subjectivity*

In the great majority of films, the line between virtue and vice is drawn quite clearly. It takes no more than a basic sense of morality for the audience to recognize which behaviors they should support and which they should reject. Yet in some stories, just as in life, this is not always so clear. Sometimes the "rightness" or "wrongness" of a value remains open to interpretation. For example, a viewer's evaluation of *One Flew Over the Cuckoo's Nest* depends upon his or her personal opinion of the controlling value of conformity. Those who consider conformity harmful may see R.P. McMurphy as a hero and Nurse Ratched as a tyrant and ogre. On the other hand, those who consider conformity a valuable social necessity may see McMurphy as a troublemaker and Nurse Ratched as a benign force for the greater good. The remainder of the audience exists somewhere in the middle, seeing good and bad in both characters. Since the story's opposing thematic values are open to such a large degree of personal subjectivity, the action found in *Cuckoo's Nest* may be interpreted in many ways. While most films end conclusively with "good" winning and "bad" losing (or vice versa), the thematic ambiguity of *Cuckoo's Nest* raises questions regarding whether or not its conclusion is just. This ambiguity is further heightened by the fact that though McMurphy fails, the film ends on an up-note with Chief's escape. Thus, the film causes the ideological debate to linger even after the credits roll. Rather than tell its audience what to think, the film encourages viewers to reflect on events, ask personal questions, and form their own conclusions.

## *Varied Degrees of Success or Failure*

Many casual moviegoers tend to lump all films into two simplistic categories: those with "happy" endings and those with "sad" endings. Either the hero lives happily ever after or meets some unfortunate demise. Yet as any storyteller should know, the feature-length cinematic structure allows for a wide variety of conclusions, each shaping the final message differently and provoking its own emotional response.

The greatest number of films end in Total Victory. Considered the stereotypical Hollywood ending, Total Victory resolves every aspect of the story in the protagonist's favor. The Story Goal is accomplished, the Internal Need is achieved, and all remaining elements are wrapped up in such a way that it indeed seems the protagonist will live happily ever after. *Star Wars, Back to the Future,* and *The Shawshank Redemption* all end this way, to name only a few examples. As the least ambiguous ending, Total Victory glorifies its thematic value more than any other. The value is upheld as absolutely righteous, something from which only good things can come. Though audiences find such conclusions the most emotionally-uplifting, the Total Victory is often criticized as unrealistic in certain contexts, and is thus not ideal for every film.

Some stories are better suited to end with the protagonist falling short of fully accomplishing his or her Story Goal. However, this is not considered a defeat as the protagonist has gained so much by the story's experience that he or she still ends up a happier or more satisfied individual. This is called Personal Victory. In *Rocky,* the title character does not win his fight against Apollo Creed, but has gained so much in other ways that it is impossible not to consider his end a happy one. In *Jerry Maguire* (1996), the protagonist does not regain the wealth and status he once had as an elite sports agent, but has gained a more fulfilling life by learning to become a selfless friend and lover.

In some instances, a Personal Victory arises as an alternative to the protagonist's original goal. In films such as *Casablanca* or *Rain Man* (1988), the protagonist originally sets a foolish or misguided goal based upon an impulse originating from his or her Fatal Flaw. When character growth occurs and the Flaw is abandoned, the protagonist realizes the original goal was wrong or short-sighted. With this, the protagonist adjusts or discards the original goal in favor of a more personally-fulfilling objective. In these cases, failure is not really a failure. By accepting change and realigning him or herself with the story world's proper value, the protagonist quits the battle in order to win the war, ending up a more complete and emotionally-satisfied individual. By putting more emphasis on character change than physical victory, a Personal Victory states that positive personal growth is more important than the petty wins or losses we may encounter in our complicated and often morally ambiguous world. Who we are is more important than what we accomplish.

The Bittersweet Victory provokes a much different emotional response. Here, the protagonist achieves victory, but at a personal price or loss that tinges the conclusion with sadness. In *Spider-Man* (2002), Peter Parker defeats the villain, but learns he must henceforth alienate himself from friends and family. In *Philadelphia* (1993), the protagonist wins his court case, but the battle has weakened him so badly that he dies soon after. In *Michael Clayton* (2007), the title character achieves justice, but at the cost of his livelihood and personal identity. Such mixed victories communicate that anything worth fighting for often comes at a price. One must make hard decisions regarding what is really important and what one is willing to lose in order to achieve it.

Further down this line we find the Pyrrhic Victory. In this case, the protagonist reaches the Story Goal, but at such an enormous cost that the victory is almost a loss in itself. *The Godfather* is a prime example. Michael Corleone accomplishes his ultimate goal, but has been forced to throw away all he once was and turn into the type of person he never wished to be. Though *The Godfather* ends in victory, it is an undeniably heartbreaking one. Such an end questions the victory and the thematic value embraced to achieve it. Was it really worth it? Could a better end have been found through other means? Or is the thematic value not all we expect it to be in such a complex and ambiguous world?

Just as there are varied degrees of victory, so there are in failure. The most common is Total Failure, in which the protagonist meets defeat in every possible way. *Chinatown, Raging Bull,* and *Citizen Kane* all conclude in this manner. By providing the ultimate punishment to those who reject the controlling value most stubbornly, Total Failure delivers the clearest condemnation of the character and his or her Fatal Flaw.

A more nuanced variety is found in Personal Failure, the mirror-opposite of Personal Victory. Here, the protagonist technically achieves his or her goal, but gains nothing from this. To the contrary, this supposed victory has only brought the protagonist harm. Like in some instances of Personal Victory, the protagonist establishes a misconceived goal stemming from the impulses of his or her Fatal Flaw. Yet in this case, the protagonist refuses to see the error of his or her ways and presses onward, escalating flawed behaviors in ways that reject what is good or meaningful and transform his or her life for the worse. In the end, the protagonist loses all to claim a meaningless prize, turning the physical victory into a personal failure. *Amadeus* provides a perfect example. Though Salieri technically achieves his goal by killing Mozart, this gains him nothing and loses him everything, from his sanity to his soul.

Bittersweet Victory also has its opposite in Bittersweet Failure. In this case, the hero fails, but in the process engenders something positive to shade the outcome with a small joy or hope for the future. *Braveheart* ends with William Wallace's execution, a failure to be certain. Yet Wallace's tragic death inspires the story's survivors to fight on, eventually winning the freedom Wallace originally sought.

It is also possible to conclude a story in a manner that is completely ambiguous. As usual, the story conflict is resolved with a climactic event (this is still a must, as any story must provide its audience with a sense of dramatic closure). However, the aftermath leaves no clear winner or loser. With no clear winner in the physical conflict, there can be no clear winner in the Thematic Argument either. This leaves the story's final message open to interpretation. Ambiguity is taken to further extremes by Mutual Annihilation. In films such as *Reservoir Dogs* (1992) or *The Departed* (2006), both sides of the dramatic conflict fail to align themselves with their story world and meet destruction in the end. With no winners and only losers, this conclusion condemns the behavior of both sides, leaving the audience at a loss for an interpretation to fill the void. Here, meaning can only be found by weighing the failures of protagonist and antagonist against a hypothetical third option that both characters chose to ignore.

## *Heroic Sacrifice*

Usually, when a story ends with the hero's death, imprisonment, or some other doomed fate, it would signify failure. However, many examples of Celebratory narratives require their heroes to commit such ultimate sacrifices. In *Saving Private Ryan* (1998), Captain Miller dies to complete his mission. In *Gladiator* (2000), Maximus surrenders his life to restore justice to Rome. In *The Dark Knight* (2008), Bruce Wayne chooses to scapegoat himself for the sake of the greater good. Despite the inherent tragedy, these conclusions are considered victories as the sacrifice allows the hero's ideals to win out in the end.

Remember that Celebratory narratives require their heroes to convert from flawed, self-interested individuals to humble servants of a greater ideal. In some cases, self-denial, self-sacrifice, or even self-annihilation is necessary to serve this ideal to its fullest. These heroes consider the ideal more important than their own lives and willingly martyr themselves for its sake. Though succumbing to death or a similar fate turns the conclusion bittersweet, a heroic sacrifice should not be considered a sad ending. As the summoned champion of the story world's controlling value, this sacrifice is the hero's destiny. While most people live their entire lives without achieving anything of greatness, these heroes make their worlds a better place through a good and noble end. Though defeated in body, these heroes are victorious in spirit.

Heroic sacrifice need not always mean physical death. The 1996 film *Slingblade* provides a good example. Its protagonist Karl is a simple-minded man released from a mental institution after twenty years of confinement. Thanks to a young boy and his good-hearted mother, Karl finds himself in an environment of love and kindness for the first time in his life. However, these good people live under the constant abuse of the mother's boyfriend Doyle. When Doyle's behavior escalates beyond control, Karl concludes that the only way to save the boy and his mother is to kill Doyle, even though this will return him to the mental institution for the rest of his life. Karl makes this sacrifice willingly. He knows he is the only person capable of ridding the world of Doyle's terror. He *must* do it to protect the people he loves. So, in a bittersweet end, Karl martyrs his freedom in service of a higher ideal.

## *Intentional Incompletion of Ending*

In some rare circumstances, the storyteller might choose to intentionally omit the story's climactic moment, leaving the final outcome a mystery. For example, *The Wrestler* (2008) cuts to black before revealing whether the protagonist survives the final event. Since the story climax completes the Thematic Argument, leaving the narrative inconclusive will also leave the theme ambiguous. One cannot even be sure if *The Wrestler* is meant to glorify the protagonist's actions with a Celebratory end or condemn them with a Cautionary one. With no resolution, we cannot tell which of the opposing values should be considered superior. We are instead expected to think about the values, weigh their benefits and drawbacks, and then decide what the conclusion should be. While some viewers may consider this a letdown in terms of plot, this device can provoke a greater thematic experience by forcing the audience to actively participate in the search for meaning rather than passively accept whatever message is provided.

## *Questioning the Resolution*

The climax has ended. The conflict has been resolved. With victory or failure, it seems the film's message has been set in stone. Or has it? Some stories add ambiguity to their themes by appearing to establish a conclusive message at the climax, only to then subvert or challenge this message in the story's epilogue. The 1960 Western *The Magnificent Seven* (as well as its Japanese original *The Seven Samurai*) ends with its heroes in victory. However, with all but three of their members slain and nothing to gain for the survivors, the heroes question whether the victory was indeed worth the price. *The Silence of the Lambs* first leads its audience to believe light has conquered the darkness, making the world a safer place. This conclusion is then subverted with a reminder that Hannibal Lecter is still running free. He could be anywhere. Possibly sitting next to you in the theater. The ambiguity of this resolution turns joy into fear, leaving the audience with mixed emotions.

1968's *Planet of the Apes* provides the most famous example. Its hero George Taylor is a cynical man who finds a new appreciation for human civilization after imprisonment by a backwards society that values ignorance over reason. By defeating the story's antagonist and escaping to freedom, Taylor seems to have struck a victory for modern man and its supposedly enlightened ways. Only this conclusion is turned on its head in the film's final moments when Taylor discovers the moldering remains of the Statue of Liberty. With this, everything is thrown into question. If Taylor's championed ideals led to the destruction of human civilization, are they really something we should value? Are the apes right to protect themselves with ignorance? By continuing to support the same values as Taylor, are we leading ourselves to our own doom?

By setting a table and then pulling the cloth from under it, these films state that there are no easy answers to life's most troubling questions. Here, victory or failure is only an illusion. The physical battle may have ended, but the thematic battle rages on. Again, the intention is to encourage the audience to think for themselves, ask questions, and come to their own conclusions; larger conclusions which extend beyond the limits of the screen.

## Zealous Overshoot

A rare and interesting form of thematic ambiguity can occur when the protagonist adopts a supposedly virtuous controlling value, but to such an extremity that this dedication turns into a new and equally destructive flaw. Just as how an airplane circling the globe to the East will eventually appear in the West, the protagonist who pursues his or her new virtue too fanatically will eventually cross a point where it turns into a vice. Though this fanaticism may allow the hero to reach his or her goal, the aftermath of such an accomplishment will create its own self-questioning resolution. *The Graduate* (1967) provides the clearest example. At its Midpoint, protagonist Ben Braddock abandons a life of superficial sex with the older Mrs. Robinson for one of true love with Robinson's daughter Elaine. When this love is threatened by a crisis event, Ben does not merely offer full commitment to the controlling value, he becomes a complete maniac for it, throwing himself over the edge with behavior that goes far beyond what should be considered reasonable. Though Ben succeeds through such madness, the victory is short-lived. It takes only moments for the audience to realize Ben's zealotry has only created more problems, raising a host of new questions as the film fades to black.

## Dual or Triple Protagonist Narratives

Some films add complexity to the basic narrative by giving equal dramatic weight to two lead characters, usually opposed to one another so that each protagonist acts as a source of conflict for the other (*Amadeus* being a prime example). This structure can be further complicated by the addition of a third protagonist in conflict with both the first and second (as seen in *American Beauty* (1999)). Stories with dual (or triple) protagonists require dual (or triple) character arcs. Each protagonist faces his or her own Crucial

Decision and must choose between accepting or rejecting of the controlling value. As usual, this decision leads to either success or failure for each protagonist at the story's end. These individual resolutions then combine to communicate the story's greater meaning. In some films, both protagonists convert, allowing the former rivals to reconcile their differences and find a mutually-satisfying conclusion. This pattern is commonly found in romances such as *When Harry Met Sally* (1989) or "buddy films" like *Toy Story* (1995) and *Lethal Weapon* (1987). Other films create a hero versus antihero dynamic where character spines are so strongly opposed that reconciliation is impossible. Here, only one side can win. In this case, only one protagonist converts (or possibly neither), allowing victory for one and failure for the other (or possibly no victory at all).

In some dual-protagonist films, the individual resolutions compliment one another. In both *Heat* (1995) and *Fargo* (1996) the law-abiding hero succeeds while the criminal antihero fails. Here, the message is clear. The righteous are rewarded while the wicked are punished. However, some films contain incompatible resolutions. In *The Departed*, both protagonists die in failure; the hero meeting a Tragic demise and the antihero a Cautionary end. These mismatched conclusions leave the story with no clear winner. With no winner, the story's message remains ambiguous. A similar ambiguity can be created when the audience is led to question the moral righteousness of one or both outcomes. *Touch of Evil* (1958) pits by-the-book lawyer Mike Vargas (the hero) against Hank Quinlan, a bordertown sheriff who uses crooked tactics to carry out the law (the antihero). Vargas ultimately wins by discrediting Quinlan and causing his death. However, the details of this resolution cause the audience to question whether this end is truly fair. Was Quinlan really a bad person for bending the law to see that justice was done? Was Vargas right to ruin Quinlan? Who really was the hero and who was the villain? Again, these lingering questions leave the resolution thematically ambiguous. This provides a richer and more nuanced end, as it once more requires the audience to think about events and weigh them ethically, perhaps even questioning their own beliefs in the process.

# ALTERNATIVE STRUCTURES

The unified structure is by far the most dominant form of narrative found in Hollywood and American Independent filmmaking. It has grown into the gold standard due to its versatility, its dependability, and most importantly its proven ability to entertain while it communicates and communicate while it entertains. However, alternatives do exist should filmmakers consider traditional methods unsuitable. Successful examples using alternative structures are quite rare. This could be for a number of reasons. Stories using alternative structures may be uncommon due to a lack of versatility. Or perhaps these forms have greater difficulty achieving the level of audience satisfaction necessary for critical or commercial success. Or it might simply be that these alternative structures have not yet had enough opportunity to perfect themselves through trial and error as the traditional structure was allowed during cinema's formative years. Nevertheless, there have been some noteworthy successes using alternative structures, making it remiss if they were not acknowledged here.

## *The God Narrative*

If there is one question that has plagued dramatists for decades, particularly regarding the seemingly-unbreakable principles of the Character Arc, it is this: "What about James Bond?" James Bond is inarguably one of the most successful movie heroes of all time, yet the character seems to ignore many of the rules attached to the traditional cinematic protagonist. First and foremost, Bond never undergoes any identifiable Character Arc. He does not experience a process of personal change, nor does he possess any clear Fatal Flaw or Internal Need. Instead, he is a perfect man, eternal and unchanging with a nature set in stone. (This excludes the more recent incarnations of the Bond franchise, starting with 2006's *Casino Royale,* which attempt to humanize the character by placing him in a more traditional mold. For this reason, these films are not included in this discussion.) This is a significant concern, seeing that the Character Arc plays a crucial role in the traditional unified structure, one that plot and theme depend upon for proper development. One must wonder why the Bond films are successful if they lack this component.

Critics may dismiss the "Bond Conundrum" by pointing out that the Bond films stand apart as an intentionally-serialized franchise, with each instance operating more like an episode of an ongoing television series than a traditional self-contained narrative. According to the argument, this requires the Bond franchise to contain a stable, unchanging cast of characters who can be placed in one adventure after another and still return to the status quo at the story's end. Unfortunately, this does not explain why the very first appearances of Bond in *Dr. No* (1962) and its follow-up *From Russia With Love* (1963) found success as stand-alone narratives. Without audience approval of these first installments, the serialized franchise could not have begun. If there is a secret to Bond's success despite its deviations from the standard rules of storytelling, it must be found in the structure of the films themselves.

To find an answer, it should first be noted that as a character James Bond does not in any way resemble a common mortal man. He is not even an exaggerated or figurative depiction of a mortal man. James Bond is superhuman. He is even more so than the likes of Superman or Hercules, as these characters still struggle with "human issues" such as internal flaws, ethical dilemmas, or personal doubts and limitations. James Bond deals with none of these. He is endlessly capable and endlessly confident. He never shows fear, never shows doubt, and never loses control of his emotions. Bond does not think, he simply acts without a moment wasted in debate.

Historically, there is another type of character who behaves this way. In mythology, stories are generally of two types (with the exception of creation or cosmological myths). The first are the hero myths in which a mortal man or woman dares challenge the power of the gods in some way. This, by various stretches of the imagination, can be considered the form the vast majority of cinematic stories follow today. The second are myths of the gods themselves in which mortals play little or no part. Often broad in scope yet shallow in meaning, these tales involve gods in conflict with other deities, supernatural creatures, or forces of nature, typically resolving in a manner that creates or restores the order of the universe.

In terms of character, James Bond has much in common with the gods depicted in myth. This is firstly due to the effortless skill with which he achieves all things. Second, the character is eternal and unchanging (the actors who play him may change, but the character essentially remains the same). Third, unlike most movie heroes, Bond has an implied immortality. In most action sequences, tension emerges from the audience's fear that the hero will meet serious harm. However, this fear is never truly present in the Bond films. The audience is always certain that Bond will find a way to survive no matter how threatening the situation. Finally and most importantly, Bond never struggles with any kind of ethical questions or moral dilemmas. He seems to instantly know what path to follow as if by supernatural instinct.

Viewed narratively, the entire Bond franchise can be likened to an eternal saga of cosmic good versus evil in which one benevolent god character continually maintains the order of the universe by keeping an endless supply of malicious deities in check. True to mythical form, Bond is aided by lesser "helper deities" such as Q, Miss Moneypenny, or various field agents; seeming immortals in their own right, often with their own quasi-superhuman abilities. The similarity to the god myth is further supported by the minimal or nonexistent presence of characters to represent everyday men or women. If they do appear, they are no more than background players with little influence upon the plot's course of events. By these similarities, it is feasible to claim that the Bond films do not follow the traditional rules of narrative structure because they abide by an alternative structure, one with a long history in myth.

Of course, more than one example is required to support this theory. God narratives are rare in the cinema, but other examples do exist. Take for instance the 1966 Western *The Good, the Bad, and the Ugly*. Its protagonist (a mysterious man known only as "Blondie") is another god-hero. Like Bond, Blondie is endlessly capable, endlessly confident, and devoid of any strong emotion or moral quandary. The fact that Blondie is a self-serving antihero is largely irrelevant. In myth, while some gods are benevolent towards mankind and others malevolent, most are completely indifferent towards humanity and act largely to serve their own needs. Indeed, Blondie behaves as if he is both outside and above the world of the common man. Their morals and concerns hold no meaning to him. His only troubles come from the story's two other larger-than-life beings; the impish trickster Tuco and the shape-shifting devil Angel Eyes (two characters with their own mirrors in mythology).

Blondie's character does not change. Like a deity, he is eternal and unchanging. This is principally because he has no need to change. Blondie's superhuman abilities make him the idealized man for his place and time. Being perfect, Blondie has no flaw to interfere with his progress, nor does he need to improve himself by seeking an Internal Need. When events do turn sour, these obstacles are only temporary. Unlike a traditional protagonist, Blondie does not need to question his behavior or seek personal change to continue his journey. He must only stay his course and the balance of the universe always returns to his side, usually by a coincidental twist of fate that suggests some cosmic order in which he holds a part.

*Forrest Gump* (1994) presents a god narrative of a far different character. *Gump* is unusual in that its narrative is structured as a saga. Rather than present the initiation and completion of a single course of dramatic events, *Gump* is composed of an episodic series of adventures with no connecting thread other than the hero's continual desire to reunite with his lost love Jenny. Like the saga created by viewing the Bond franchise as a whole or the suggested adventures Blondie has had and will continue to have after the events of *The Good, the Bad & the Ugly*, there is something mythical about this structure. Forrest Gump is an "immortal" whose adventures seem to stretch across time without end.

It might seem strange to consider Forrest a god-hero, yet he demonstrates the same non-traditional qualities found in Blondie or James Bond. First, Forrest perpetually exists outside of the world of the common man. He may walk among them, but he is not one of them. Thanks to his pure heart and simple mind, Forrest is elevated into a virtuous being who cannot lie, cannot hate, and cannot understand the petty prejudices that taint those around him. He can almost be considered a being without sin. Second, Forrest's physical abilities border on the supernatural. He has the speed to become a college football All-American. He has the strength to carry five Army buddies to safety. He becomes a world-class ping pong champion within months of picking up a paddle. Third, he has an implied immortality, not only in body (he survives Vietnam and one of the most devastating hurricanes in history) but also in spirit. As decades pass, Forrest finds himself connected to nearly every major cultural event as if he were some cosmic thread uniting American history. Fourth and most importantly, Forrest never suffers from any kind of ethical or moral dilemma. He does not think. He simply acts and always comes out in the right.

Forrest Gump does not have any Fatal Flaw he must overcome. Though his childlike nature causes difficulty at times, this is not a Flaw in the traditional sense. First, this quality is innate and thus cannot be changed. Second, this "flaw" is actually Forrest's greatest virtue as it continually leads him down the correct path no matter the circumstance. Like Bond and Blondie, Forrest Gump has no need to change and therefore has no Character Arc.

The Bond franchise, *The Good, the Bad and the Ugly,* and *Forrest Gump* provide three examples of highly-successful films of nontraditional structure in which the protagonists share the same unusual traits. These successes are not freak occurrences, but evidence of an alternate structural form, one with significant parallels in the god narratives of myth. Further investigation will be needed to uncover the details by which this structure operates. Hopefully, future analysis will reveal how storytellers may intentionally implement this structure with the same consistency as the traditional structural form.

## The Non-Narrative and Anti-Narrative

Broadly speaking, the non-narrative and anti-narrative are forms of cinema which intentionally disregard, alter, or subvert the tendencies of traditional storytelling for the sake of artistic expression. Considered to exist within the vaguely-defined realm of "art cinema," both are set apart by the intentional act of experimentation upon the narrative form. By eschewing the established norms of mainstream filmmaking, these films test the limits of the cinematic medium to explore its broader range of expression. This technically means the "art film" has no rules except for those the artist chooses to apply. Therefore, we cannot assign any specific guidelines to the non-narrative or anti-narrative forms, but speak only of their general tendencies.

The term "non-narrative" is a misnomer. These films do contain narratives. As long as one event leads to another, a narrative will exist. This label instead implies the intentional de-emphasis of plot in order to focus more attention upon character or theme. As stated in Chapter 1-3, traditional storytelling uses plot as a Trojan Horse. The unified narrative structure grasps the viewer's attention with dramatic action in order to communicate a message within. However, audiences are often so distracted by the entertainment that they overlook the message. Depending on the artist's intentions, he or she may find it preferable to forefront the film's message through more direct means rather than hide it behind the mechanics of plot.

The non-narrative film draws attention away from plot through the intentional use of an incomplete or nonexistent Story Spine. The narrative may lack a definite Story Problem or Story Goal. There may be no central dramatic conflict. In some cases, these elements may be present, but the protagonist's behaviors do not follow a clear Path of Action. The film may even disregard the concept of a central protagonist altogether. With no unified spine of events, the elements of character and theme become the principle carriers of meaning. (Although one must be warned that by eliminating the influence of the Story Spine, the Character Arc and Thematic Argument will no longer develop in the same manner found in a traditional unified narrative. Hence, these films must rely on nontraditional structures for character and theme or may contain no structure at all.)

Traditional cinematic storytelling uses the unified narrative structure to present a simplified world in which every action has a purpose and all events lead to a conclusive end. While this provides a clear and effective story, it does not accurately reflect experiences encountered in real life. By down-playing or ignoring the Story Spine, the non-narrative is able to present a greater semblance of reality. This is the non-narrative's greatest strength. The obvious downside is the loss of audience participation that can come from tightly-structured plot events. A traditional film turns viewership into an interactive experience. The plot raises questions and baits the audience with information, encouraging viewers to predict what might occur next. The non-narrative does not allow such participation. Its deliberate lack of plot resigns viewers to the lesser role of detached observers. This requires much more patience on the part of the audience. Unfortunately, many casual moviegoers lack such patience, hence the low commercial appeal of these films and the rarity with which they are produced in the Hollywood system.

The anti-narrative presents filmmaking at its most experimental. While the non-narrative is still largely a story-based experience, the anti-narrative rejects story as the primary carrier of meaning by intentionally violating or disregarding the basic principles of narrative itself. Fundamentals such as causality, linearity, dramatic unity, or even character may be missing from these films. The anti-narrative instead prefers to communicate directly through the physical properties of the medium; that is, the explicit use of image, sound, and montage in a decidedly non-narrative form. The anti-narrative can be thought of as the cinematic equivalent of an abstract painting. Whereas traditional storytelling communicates through a linear logic that shows how one action leads directly to the next, the content of an anti-narrative must often be evaluated collectively, like objects in a collage. The audience compares and contrasts the various actions, images, and sounds in relation to one another and like the viewer of an abstract painting, extracts a meaning from the whole.

By ignoring the basic principles of narrative, the anti-narrative often turns viewership into a jarring, disorientating, or even incomprehensible experience. Therefore, it goes without saying that the anti-narrative is primarily used for artistic expression rather than anything resembling commercial entertainment. Furthermore, anti-narratives are typically far more successful as short films than features. True feature-length anti-narratives are extremely rare. This is chiefly because anti-narratives require so much mental effort on the part of the audience that they become difficult, if not impossible to follow for an extended length of time. Even the most successful proponents of anti-narrative such as David Lynch (*Lost Highway, Mulholland Drive, Inland Empire*) or Richard Linklater (*Slacker, Waking Life*) alternate between narrative and anti-narrative within their films to provide a lifeboat of coherence within a sea of abstraction.

Since the content and composition of the anti-narrative falls far outside the traditional boundaries of screencraft, we will end our discussion here. In fact, it is debatable as to whether anything resembling a screenplay can be written for an anti-narrative film. Since these films far more resemble audio-visual art than anything in the realm of storytelling, the anti-narrative's ultimate form depends more upon the work of camera and editing than anything that can be adequately captured on the printed page.

## The Multi-Narrative

The multi-narrative is more popularly known as the ensemble film. However, this term can be confusing. "Ensemble" was originally used as a promotional term to indicate a film with a large cast of recognizable actors rather than a single leading man or woman (one of the best early examples being 1932's *Grand Hotel*). However, a true "ensemble film" requires more than a large cast. Its distinguishing trait is the presence of multiple storylines (from as few as three to up to a dozen), each with its own protagonist and individual premise. For the most part, these lines of narrative develop independently from one another as if they were separate films. Hence the more accurate term "multi-narrative." It is one film containing many stories. Noteworthy recent examples include *Magnolia* (1999), *Traffic* (2000), and *Crash* (2004).

Structurally, the multi-narrative presents its many lines of action in parallel. Rather than follow a single story for an extended length of time, the film alternates from one to the next, giving the impression of simultaneous action. This way, each line develops concurrently with the others. The experience is not unlike watching several films at once on television with the viewer changing channels at the end of each sequence. The greatest challenge with a multi-narrative lies in finding the proper balance and organization between the various storylines so that each develops at the same pace without any one line overshadowing the others while still maintaining an overall sensation of dramatic rise and fall.

This form is not unique to cinema. Multi-protagonist novels are fairly common. Unfortunately, unlike the novel with its unlimited length, a cinematic multi-narrative must deal with restrictions regarding what can be reasonably accomplished within the limits of a single feature film. As usual, restrictions necessitate structure. In terms of development, each line of action in the multi-narrative follows the same basic structure found in a traditional film. In each, the protagonist has a Story Spine with a personal Problem and Goal, undergoes a Character Arc, and takes part in the ideological battle between the theme and anti-theme. At some point, each protagonist faces a Crucial Decision where he or she must either convert to the story world's supported value or reject it in favor of his or her Fatal Flaw, leading to either success or failure at the storyline's end. If one were to re-edit a multi-narrative so that each line could be viewed independently, one would find that each story stands on its own as a traditionally-structured narrative. The only difference would be far less development in terms of plot and character. By increasing the *scope* of the film to include multiple storylines, the multi-narrative must reduce the *scale* of each storyline lest the film greatly exceed its prescribed length. With less room for development, each Story Spine and Character Arc must often be stripped down to their most important structural moments.

As if structuring multiple storylines were not enough of a challenge, a multi-narrative presents the storyteller with an even more significant problem. How can a film with many lines of action still provide its audience with a coherently unified experience? Though separate, the various storylines must contain an element of cohesion that binds them together as a single film with a single thematic message. Without this connection, the film's content will feel random and arbitrary, confusing the audience with many possible messages which may hold no relevancy to one another.

Some multi-narratives achieve unification through plot. Storylines are interwoven so that actions performed in one line exert an influence upon one or more of the others. This way, the lines are not separate, but part of an interconnected web, forming a super-structure or "over-narrative." Some multi-narratives interweave their lines more tightly than others. In *Magnolia*, *Crash*, and *Grand Hotel*, each protagonist also appears as a supporting character in one or more of the other lines of action. This intertwines the fates of the many characters, suggesting that they are all participants in a greater scheme of events. When executed more loosely, a shared premise, location, or physical object may maintain an indirect connection between narrative lines. For example, *Traffic* uses the multi-narrative to explore the broad premise of the war on drugs. Its four storylines, while only marginally related to one another in terms of plot, remain connected in that each examines a more specific aspect of this complex social issue. *Nashville* (1975) uses time and place to unify its threads. All of its characters have gathered at a single location to take part in a single event. This brings all lines of action together at the story's end to provide a unified conclusion. While disconnected, each narrative contributes a part to the greater story behind this event.

However, such devices of plot are not an absolute requirement. Of all narrative elements which might act to unify the disparate lines of action, the most important is theme. Thematically, the multi-narrative presents many stories about the same thing. While the contents of each storyline may differ drastically, the thematic battle essentially remains the same. Each scenario presents a unique conflict orientated around the same theme and anti-theme. When combined, the many stories form the film's Thematic Argument as a whole.

Here we find the great advantage the multi-narrative holds over a traditional film. The exploration of theme is not limited to the experiences of one character. It is instead examined through many different perspectives in many different contexts. Whereas a single-protagonist narrative can only provide one argument for or against the story's thematic value, the multi-narrative does the work of many films, turning the Thematic Argument into a genuinely multi-sided debate. As the multi-narrative develops, some protagonists choose to align themselves with the theme and some with the anti-theme. Because of this, some succeed while others fail. The meaning suggested by each individual resolution is not conclusive in its own right, but contributes a part to the film's greater thematic whole. By observing many outcomes issuing from the same Thematic Argument, the audience receives a far broader and more well-rounded evaluation of the film's central value.

## *The Omnibus Narrative*

The omnibus narrative bears many similarities to the multi-narrative. Both present multiple storylines orientated around the same Thematic Argument. The key difference is in structure and presentation. While the multi-narrative develops its various lines in parallel, the omnibus uses an episodic format. Generally speaking, the omnibus operates like a series of short films. One storyline begins, develops to a conclusion, and then ends. A new storyline then begins and repeats this process.

Like the multi-narrative, the omnibus originated in literature. It is not unusual to find a novel composed of multiple short stories which may or may not feature shared characters, premises, or locations, yet nevertheless address a single unifying theme. This episodic form gives the storyteller much greater freedom. Each of the shorts may feature the same cast or they may not. Their plots may be connected, or may have nothing physically in common. Even the rules of time and space are less rigid as the stories need not occur in chronological order or even exist in the same reality.

The most well-known example of a cinematic omnibus is 1994's *Pulp Fiction. Pulp Fiction* created a great stir upon its release for what seemed like such a unique and innovative structure. Yet in truth, filmmaker Quentin Tarantino simply took the omnibus format found in literature and adapted it to the screen. Each segment of *Pulp Fiction* operates like an individual short film. Being independent stories, each follows the basic unified structure as if they were stand-alone narratives, albeit minimized on account of length.

In each segment, a character has a problem and a goal, a need and a flaw. At some point, the character faces a Crucial Decision where he or she either realigns with the story world's controlling value or rejects it.* This culminates in a dramatic resolution which allows the segment to end and the next to begin.

Just like in the multi-narrative, these many stories cannot be a random collection of unrelated episodes. No coherent meaning can be gained by that. Again, the omnibus uses multiple conflicts and situations to tell many stories about the same thing, unifying the entire work under a single Thematic Argument. In *Pulp Fiction,* each segment presents a crisis whereby a character must choose between continuing his selfish, evil ways or accepting a responsibility as a "shepherd of the weak." Cohesion is further achieved by the inclusion of shared characters and related incidents within each narrative. Omnibus films fail when their segments lack such physical or ideological connections. Rather than create a cohesive film, they provide only two hours of disconnection. In contrast, a successful omnibus presents a unified work in which the whole is greater than the sum of its parts. While each segment may provide a portion of meaning on its own, a greater meaning is formed by comparing and contrasting the events of the many stories to one another. Through this combination of characters, conflicts, and dramatic outcomes, the viewer receives a multifaceted perspective upon the central value, resulting in a thematic debate of much greater breadth than that found in a single-narrative film.

* In examples such as *Pulp Fiction* where the same characters appear in more than one segment, the course of character change may be spread across the length of the film. Often, the conflict of one segment initiates character transformation and the conflict of a later segment completes it.

# CONCLUSION TO PART I

"That's it?" you may ask. "It's that simple?" The unified narrative structure —the structure behind all other structures—the principles guiding all other principles—the shared thread that unites every traditionally-told Hollywood and American Independent film—boils down to something that seems so basic? The answer, in a nutshell, is yes. It is nothing short of amazing that this one simple structure, endlessly repeated, could be the single source of the countless films we all love and enjoy. Yet this is indeed the case. Every great Hollywood or American Independent story is essentially the same regardless of content, style, tone, or ideological intent.

However, what might be most amazing is that every one of these stories seem so different to the viewer. The fact that cinematic stories can all be the same yet at the same time infinitely different seems paradoxical. Yet this paradox can be dispelled if one compares storytelling to the many other complex systems of phenomena found in our natural world. From Isaac Newton's Three Laws of Motion to Charles Darwin's Evolution by Natural Selection, everything encountered in the known universe originates from, and can be understood by the most basic of principles. Simple rules create balance and order. Simplicity in principle allows for complexity in execution. Simplicity equals strength. From this starting point, the possibilities expand without limit. Yet these principles exist for legitimate reasons. Chapter 1-2 established that the cinematic medium imposes limits upon its storytelling. It also established that audiences have certain psychological needs. On top of this, a story must fulfill its artistic purpose of creative communication. The basic unified structure is so successful because it satisfies all of these requirements while still providing the storyteller with a wide enough flexibility to create nearly any kind of story expressing nearly any kind of personal meaning. The unified narrative structure ensures that a cinematic story does what it *needs* to do while giving the storyteller the freedom to do what he or she *wants* to do.

Once again, no one invented this unified structure. It was not contrived by critics or analysts and forced upon its medium. It developed naturally in response to the needs of the audience, artist, and cinematic form. Those films that gravitated towards its principles were rewarded with recognition and success. Those that did not were banished to obscurity. This structure was not created so much as it evolved. It was not discovered so much as it discovered itself. In this way, the cinematic story found its most perfect form, one capable of satisfying audiences again and again without straying from its functional necessities. This structure is the reason why the magic of movies has not waned after a hundred years. Every well-told cinematic narrative is built on a solid foundation that fulfills the intellectual, emotional, ideological, and technical requirements of great storytelling while still holding infinite possibilities for individual artistic expression.

Yet on the other hand, cinematic storytelling is not so simple. Far from it. Though narrative structure provides an essential part of the cinematic experience, it does not create a great story on its own. Structure provides shape, but not substance. Even when perfectly executed, a story is worth little unless its content is also found to be *meaningful*. Structure may provide a process through which meaning is communicated, but it does not provide any meaning in and of itself. This comes from a much deeper source.

Part II of this book will explore these deeper sources of meaning. Stories are created for reasons that go far beyond mere entertainment. Throughout history, storytelling has served humanity's most basic psychological and sociological needs by giving our world a sense of balance, order, and meaning. Part II examines how this is accomplished, both in terms of story's basic origins and the manner which these processes have evolved to create the complex and sophisticated modes of expression found in the cinema today.

# APPENDIX

*Screenwriting Down to the Atoms: The Absolute Essentials Edition* is available for download from the following online retailers:

Amazon.com
*http://www.amazon.com/books*

Apple iBook Store
*available through the iBook app for Apple devices*

Baker & Taylor's Blio.com
*http://www.blio.com*

Barnes & Noble Nook Store
*http://nook.barnesandnoble.com*

Kobo
*http://www.kobo.com*

Oyster Books
*https://www.oysterbooks.com/*

Smashwords
*https://www.smashwords.com/*

*Michael Welles Schock was born in Nebraska, educated in Los Angeles, and currently resides in Portland, Oregon. He writes on screencraft and practical narrative theory. Michael Welles Schock is also the author of* Screenwriting Down to the Atoms, *a guide for beginning and intermediate screenwriters published in 2013.*

*contact: scriptmonk@scriptmonkindustries.com*
*http://www.scriptmonkindustries.com*